CODE BLUE

Serious Matters
of the Heart

BISHOP
DONALD R. DOWNING, DR.

Treasure House

An Imprint of

Destiny Image® Publishers, Inc.

P.O. Box 310
Shippensburg, PA 17257-0310

"For where your treasure is, there will your heart be also."
Matthew 6:21

ISBN 0-7684-2970-6

For Worldwide Distribution
Printed in the U.S.A.

This book and all other Destiny Image, Revival Press, MercyPlace, Fresh Bread, Destiny Image Fiction, and Treasure House books are available at Christian bookstores and distributors worldwide.

1 2 3 4 5 6 7 8 9 10 / 09 08 07 06 05 04

For a U.S. bookstore nearest you, call
1-800-722-6774.

For more information on foreign distributors, call
717-532-3040.

Or reach us on the Internet:
www.destinyimage.com

CODE BLUE

ACKNOWLEDGMENTS

I give honor and thanks to my Lord and Savior for the revelation of Code Blue, the understanding of Code Red, and the strength to write this book. Thanks to Mrs. Porcia Hardy for the many hours of typing and content editing, as well as for her words of encouragement. Thanks to Mrs. Betty Carroll for her typing, prayers, and faith in God. Thanks to Mrs. Nellena Coley and Debra Spearman for their content editing, careful overview, and Christian love. Thanks to the multi-talented Bishop Myles Spires who placed the "finishing touch" on each page of this book with wisdom and blessings for the Body of Christ. Thanks to Elder Yvette Carter and Ron Kenolly. To my dear wife and family, my brothers and sisters who prayed for me during my darkest hours in ministry when I was so low that I had to look up to see the ground. To Dr. Fred Price and Creflo Dollar, men who taught me how to walk in the faith of God, and to evangelist R.W. Schambch who preached the fear of God into my soul. To my church family, pastors, and ministers, who spoke the word of prophecy that did come to pass. To the Downing family—I'm proud to be your brother. I thank all of you with all of my heart.

Bishop Donald R. Downing

TABLE OF CONTENTS

FOREWORD

"What lies behind us and what lies before us are just tiny matters compared to what lies within us."

~ Oliver Wendell Holmes

Until man comes to know the heart of the Cross, he cannot have a right relationship and fellowship with the God of the Cross. None can see the Lord unless he first sees the heart of the Cross. The wounded and broken heart of the Lamb of God was perfect, pure, and clean but was made sinful, defiled, and detestable that we may be made holy, pure, and approved. Our connection to God through the cross of Christ is that of the heart. We can only know God by those things that flow out of His heart, producing God-consciousness, a new life, and a holy lifestyle. Our heart determines who we really are, and one can only be in God's presence if his heart is.

In June 1990, God spoke life-changing words to my heart that redefined my ministry, doctrine, and theology forever. He asked me the following three questions: "Have you seen the hearts of the twelve apostles?" "Have you seen the hearts of my servants Moses, David, and Abraham?" To these first two questions, I responded, "No, Lord." Then God asked me the final question—"Have you seen My Heart?" Immediately shame, guilt, and conviction flooded my being. Tears flowed from my eyes. "What's the matter, Lord?" I cried. "I'm a new testament believer. I believe in your Son, Jesus Christ. I hold to the apostles' doctrine; I'm faithful to your Word. I pray, walk by faith, and love you will all of my heart. Why should I see their hearts?" God revealed to me that the Bible, God's revealed Word to mankind, was heart-designed to dwell in the heart of the believer. The condition of man's heart determines his eternal resting place. Nothing—not doctrine, theology, or works—is as serious as the condition of man's heart. As I reflected on God's word, I came to the conclusion that man's heart condition is a very serious matter. Our heart is the key to the gates of heaven or the fiery doors of hell.

I earnestly began to search the Scriptures to learn more about the heart and came to the understanding that the heart rules the past, controls the present, and determines the future. My first surprise came when I encountered Genesis 6:5-7 and discovered that it was the "thoughts and imaginations of man's heart" that caused the flood—not just sin alone! There is no scripture in the Bible that clearly states that sin caused the flood. I fell on my knees in worship and sought the Lord about this matter. God spoke the following words to my spirit: "*Teacher, my son, if the purpose of the flood that I did send upon the earth was to remove all sin, then I failed. Is there any failure in me?*" He asked. "Oh, no Lord," I said out loud. He replied, "*I am a God of the heart, and every issue or controversy I have with mankind, either for them or against them, is due to the total condition of the intents and contents of their hearts. Man did grieve Me in my heart; therefore, I brought forth total destruction.*" Immediately I realized that God is a God of the heart, and everything of the heart is a serious matter—even to the eternal. Like many Christians, I had become so absolute in God's Word to the point that I existed in an obsolete state of understanding God's will, hearing His voice, and recognizing the revelations of the heart.

A vision then came into my spirit of a farmer with many acres of apple trees, far too many to count. Each apple tree had more apples than any tree could possibly bear, but upon closer inspection every apple was rotten and worthless. Tears flowed from the farmer's eyes as he looked upon his worthless, defiled apple orchard, which he had so carefully planted. "What a loss,"

I thought. "Such a great waste of time and labor. What can the farmer do?" I asked out loud. For the last time that day, God spoke saying; "*Don, I am that farmer in grief. The trees are men. The rotten apples are the fruit of their labor (sin); however, in error you see only the rotten fruit (sin). Now you must see and understand that it's the condition of the heart of the trees (man) that produced the rotten fruit and, if allowed to continue, each year the apple trees would bring forth fruit more rotten than the previous crop. The farmer must destroy every tree because of the condition of the heart and not just its rotten fruit. I brought forth the flood, but it shall be fire at the end of time. For I will judge and do judge the condition of men's hearts. Even My people, who are called by My name, still make Me grieve within My heart. They refuse to know Me, serve Me, and give Me all of their hearts. I am a God of the heart, and I am a serious God. All the works of My hands, My word, My laws, and My commandments are very serious matters to consider. I am grieved at My heart, My eyes are still tearful, and My heart still hurts for so many of My people for they know not me. Go forth now—write, teach, preach, and tell My people about their hearts. Tell them that I am a God of the heart. Sin is no longer the key issue of concern; their heart is. The death of My Son on Calvary has paid for all sin. Warn them, for I do come quickly to give unto mankind according to all of the counsels of their hearts.*" "Yes, Lord!" I shouted.

With deep concern, I realized in my spirit that I, too, was among the many thousands of individuals who still looked on the "outward appearance" and not on the heart. I was out of focus with God's purpose. I needed desperately to see what God saw within me so I would know what God wanted me to know about myself. My doctrine and theology needed to be upgraded to include concepts and revelations of the heart so that I might inwardly know, understand, and meet the requirement of my destiny. I realized that I must seek God's face to discover His heart. If I was to dwell in the heart of God as He dwelled in my heart, I needed to see through His eyes, hear through His ears, speak by His mouth, and walk daily in His footsteps.

I stood on my feet and remembered what King David said about the heart's condition in the book of Psalms. Psalm 51:10

11

says, "Create in me a clean heart, O God; and renew a right spirit within me." In Psalm 19:14, he wrote, "Let the words of my mouth, and the meditation of my heart, be acceptable in thy sight, O Lord, my strength, and my redeemer." And in Psalm 119:11, he says, "Thy word have I hid in mine heart, that I might not sin against Thee."

I found out that the kingdom of God is within me (Luke 17:21); that my body is the temple of the Most High God, and I therefore must not defile it (1 Corinthians 3:16-17); that I am bought with a price (1 Corinthians 6:19-20); and that I am to seek first the kingdom of God and His righteousness (Matthew 6:33). God wanted me to look and seek my inner man—my heart, His dwelling place—that I may know Him and find Him and then also find my new man. Man's requirements are not always God's will. I learned that if I am to excel in Christ as God's servant, I must be a servant in my heart, not just for outward appearance's sake. I can never be any more than my heart is.

God is truly a "God of the heart." God views my thoughts and imaginations, which are produced by the contents, intents and motives, of my heart, as the root of sin, not just the sinful acts of my flesh as I had previously believed. Acts 8:18-23 tells us about Simon the Sorcerer, who wanted to pay the disciples to give him power to lay hands upon someone that they would receive the Holy Spirit. Peter told Simon to ask God to forgive him for his thoughts. I realized that I needed to do the same. While we ask God to forgive us for our sins, it is also very important that we repent of our evil thoughts and wicked imaginations.

I believe that the heart's motives and intents can bind a believer in a Code Red state of sin. God sees the thoughts and the imaginations of the heart. One may be sitting in a Bible study group, church service, or in the midst of a sermon when sinful thoughts appear and place him or her in danger of Code Blue. Therefore, I encourage all believers to become extremely serious about their hearts and to seek to know their true inward condition. We each must focus on a new objective—knowing the heart of God. He that creates is always greater than that which is created. I pray that this book will help you know the Lord of the heart in a new and exciting way.

1

SERIOUS MATTERS OF THE HEART

1 Peter 3:4: *"But let it be the hidden man of the heart, in that which is not corruptible, even the ornament of a meek and quiet spirit, which is in the sight of God of great price."*

When we mention the word "heart," one might think about the inward organ fixed within our physical frame that beats 60-80 times per minute. Webster's dictionary defines the term "heart" as "the center, vital, or innermost part—the very core." From Genesis to Revelation, the Bible gives us the true definition and understanding of our heart as the center of life and the place where God dwells! Our innermost thoughts, feelings, and consciousness are contained in our hearts. In essence, the heart is the information center and the sphere of divine influence. Our scripture reference above refers to "the hidden man of the heart," which is the eternal spirit man unseen by the natural eye.

The heart is also a reproductive system that works to reproduce all of the desires that it contains. In anger, the heart is out of control; in forgetfulness, the heart loses its direction; in resentment, the heart becomes bitter; in laziness, the heart becomes fat, idle and slothful; in despair, the heart becomes anxious. When we're rude, the heart becomes disrespectful; in sorrow, the heart is sad, downcast, and full of grief. It may be divided, it has a door, has tables, it may hold error, walk after the flesh, go back into the world, sin again, be foolish, experience failure, control one's footsteps, cause preachers to preach the wrong sermon, and lead many to join the wrong church for all the wrong reasons.

But when the heart is working to its full capacity and potential, it produces many positives. In loyalty, the heart is positive, certain, and sure; in patience, the heart is strengthened, grows more tolerant, and grows in endurance; in mercy, the heart is guided by compassion, favor, and grace; in grace, pity comes forth and the heart is easily touched; in ability, the heart excels over its enemies, shows its strength, and demonstrates its great character; in peace, the heart finds rest and contentment; in respect, it produces honor and virtue; and in joy, the heart rejoices in God the Savior.

The heart is the catalyst for all true prayer, praise, and worship. In prayer, believers make their desires known to God by entering into His presence with thanksgiving in their hearts; in praise the heart magnifies and glorifies a worthy God; and in worship the heart acknowledges God for who He is. We have the power to open our heart, set our heart, and make serious heart decisions. God knows the intents and contents of our hearts and is always testing it. Because He is our spiritual physician, He wants to reveal to us His diagnostic analysis of the condition of our heart and the spiritual medication (love) that is mandatory to fix it when necessary.

While in the midst of intense worship and praise, in Bible study, or even while we are working at our jobs, often unbeknownst to us, the heart may be proclaiming a good or evil matter. Psalm 45:1 says, "My heart is inditing [composing/writing] a good matter."

The heart may produce tears, grieve even while one's lips are smiling, lead the soul to eternal condemnation, hold doubt and unbelief, make serious spiritual decisions without one's knowledge, think evil in the midst of praise and worship, anger, and, for the lost, be a dwelling place for demons. It controls a person's footsteps, it may commune with God while one sleeps, may be far from God or lie to God. It may search for God, sing to God, or offend God on a daily basis.

The heart may be prideful or judgemental, suggest immoral ideas, work iniquity, and hold on to God while yet trying to turn from God. It may repent or give tithes and offering while murmuring and complaining. It may act single and yet be legally married.

The heart watches and knows you. It may be tested, approved, or disapproved by God. For those in leadership the heart may determine church growth and weekly church attendance. It may be blinded, jealous, and filled with trash, lust and fear. It holds the breath of life; it is the seat of change and thought; and it may voice its opinion regardless of the occasion. It even determines how much we eat. Whatever our heart contains is a serious matter, for the heart is deceitful above all things (Jeremiah 17:9-10). When our spiritual arteries become clogged due to doubt and unbelief, we must run to Christ, the Great Heart Physician. We must lay upon His bed of love, asking Him to check our hearts with His "Word" stethoscope, and if there is any Code Blue, use His spiritual defilberator, the Holy Spirit, to restore the heart. Christ is our only true heart helper. Even the Bible, God's ordained Word, has no effect without Christ dwelling within our hearts.

Needless to say, I was troubled about the condition of my own heart as I read Matthew 5:8, that only the "pure in heart" shall see God. "But what if my heart isn't pure," I wondered. Well the answer was obvious—I would not see God!

THE HIDDEN MAN OF THE HEART

For many years, I thought the heart was synonymous with the spirit. However, in Luke 16:19-31, the Lord tells the story of a wicked-hearted rich man and Lazarus, the poor beggar who laid at his gate, hungry and full of sores. Both had died—the rich man went to hell while Lazarus rested in Abraham's bosom. The fleshly bodies of both were still upon the earth, decaying in a graveyard, while their spirits were locked in eternity. The hearts of both of these men had sealed their destiny. While in hell, the rich man remembered his brothers were not saved and requested something be done about it. In this scripture, we see that the rich man had all of his faculties including spiritual eyes, hands, arms, and feet. He could speak, think, remember, and hold a common conversation. Yet we know that his natural body remained in a casket upon the earth while his heart had taken him into an eternal place, separated from God forever. This is a serious matter.

I would dare say that the spirit man, the hidden man in our hearts, is more valuable and precious than all of the riches and cares of this world. It is crucial that we give God all of our heart today, for the heart determines if a soul will rest in heaven or hell. (See Proverbs 23:26.)

God chose our hearts for His dwelling place because it was the best place to sow all of the attributes of Himself. Jesus Christ, the Word of God, is also the God of our heart. His inward dwelling, power, and presence protect, preserve, fix, repair, and keep our hearts.

The Body of Christ in these last days must seriously address holiness, righteousness, a pure heart, agape love, and faith. What we allow to exist in our hearts determines the quality of our spiritual walk of faith, relationship, and fellowship with God. How do we expect to give perfect praise unto God with an imperfect heart? Does God dwell in imperfect places? Can we live in perfect peace, showing perfect love without a perfect heart? The answer is a resounding no! 1 Corinthians 2:6 states: "Howbeit we speak wisdom among them that are perfect: yet not the wisdom of this world, nor of the princes of this world, that come to nought." Matthew 5:48 says: "Be ye therefore perfect, even as your Father which is in heaven is perfect." In Psalm 37:37, we read, "Mark the perfect man, and behold the upright; for the end of that man is peace." (See also John 17:23 and Job 1:1,8 for more on this subject.) Automatically we translate the word perfect to mean "spiritually mature," but God is perfect and not spiritually mature, and He will not dwell within an imperfect temple. Let's be serious. God spends His time looking throughout the earth for perfect hearts. 2 Chronicles 16:9 says, "For the eyes of the Lord run to and fro throughout the whole earth, to show himself strong in the behalf of them whose heart is perfect toward him. Herein thou hast done foolishly: therefore from henceforth thou shalt have wars."

Just as God is focused upon all serious matters, so should we be. We can and must be all that the Word of God says we are. Howbeit, it seems that material things such as money, houses, automobiles, society, and the work place supersede that which matters to God. We still sin knowing its costly price. We tell lies while knowing God's opinion of it. We systematically rob God in our tithes and offerings and refuse to love our neighbors as we love ourselves. Regardless of the titles we carry, what church we belong to, or our special gifts and callings, it's the condition of our hearts that concerns God most. Why? No title given or written is greater than the heart. It is the heart that makes the title valid in God's presence. There are many gifts and fruits of the Spirit, yet all must be heart-seeded, ruled, and operated.

Let us ask ourselves some serious questions right now—are we doing God's perfect will from the heart? Or are we doing our own will, wanting God to be there when we need Him? What is God's desire for our lives versus our own desire? What's in our hands must never be held as greater in power and value than what God has placed within our hearts.

WE MUST BE HEART-FOCUSED AND DESTINY-MINDED

Let every believer view a matter and rightly determine if it's holy or unholy, if it's right or wrong, and whether the end result will be a blessing or a curse. It is time to cease committing immoral acts in our heart, flesh, and thought patterns. We need to know the truth, whether we're heaven-ready or hell-bound. The condition of our heart determines both. But we say that we haven't committed any acts of sin—physically! The Lord reveals to us in Matthew 5:28: "But I say unto you, That whosoever looks on a woman to lust after her hath already committed adultery with her *in his heart*" (emphasis added). What? Does this saying of Christ mean that we can commit a sin, even adultery, within our spirit man and not just bodily? The answer is "Yes!" Through this scripture, we can conclude that it is not the acts of the flesh that determines the sin, but the inward status of the heart. God is focused on our heart's motives, intents, thoughts,

19

and imaginations, and by them He determines the sin. Most Christians are flesh-focused and sin-conscious while God is heart-focused and destiny-minded. It's time for us to focus where God is focused that we may see exactly what He sees, and He's looking inwardly at our hearts.

Needless to say, the heart reveals our true character, for as a man thinks in his heart, so is he. Therefore, we must conclude that our actions or lack thereof don't always reveal our true state of righteousness within.

One Sunday morning as I watched a Christian broadcast, I marveled at the great words each speaker used to proclaim the gospel. Some of them spoke with such power and faith that I found myself dancing and shouting in the middle of the living room floor. After it was all over, a still, small voice spoke within my heart saying *"Don, just because one is eloquent of speech doesn't always mean that they are eloquent in heart. Many will say one thing out of their mouth but mean another thing in their heart. For some that you have seen confess Me greatly but possess me poorly."* Immediately in a vision, I saw the deceitful, lying, lustful, covetous, and lost hearts sitting in the pews and the rebellious and disobedient hearts sitting as kings ruling from the pulpit. I was troubled in my spirit all the day long, for I realized that words from the mouth of many ministers are not from the heart of God, neither are they always a result of the will of God. Surely we need the mercies of God's grace. It's a serious matter of the heart.

God wants us to know our heart and tries fervently to reveal it unto us. We must become more heart-conscience if we're to remain heart-connected with God. Perhaps our heart has been separated from the will and purposes of God through procrastination, slothfulness, backbiting, rebelliousness, or lack of knowledge. Now is the appointed time for every Christian to know the contents of his or her own heart so that none be disconnected from God's purpose. To avoid inward spiritual pollution and defilement, a daily heart presentation unto God is highly recommended. Yes, it's time for us to have a spiritual heart inspection. He is our great Heart Inspector, Heart Fixer, Preserver, and Mind Regulator.

Many serious matters are before us, and they are deeply rooted within the heart. Whether it's evil or good, we must correctly identify the source, purpose, work, and end result within the heart. Everything we encounter produces results—the smallest thing sown within our heart may bring about Code Blue death and mass destruction. A little leaven leavens the whole lump. Most things have the ultimate power to change our heart and affect our lives if they become seeded, rooted, and left to their own devices within our heart.

God is a God of prayer. We serve not only a "prayer answering" God, but a "praying" God. We serve a God that is praying continuously for His people. And just as we desire that He answers our prayers; He desires that His prayers be answered through us. Consider Luke 22:32: "But I have prayed for thee, that thy faith fail not; and when thou art converted, strengthen thy brethren."

The Lord hears what we pray, so why don't we hear what He's praying? Don't you realize that Jesus Christ is praying for every serious matter within the earthly realm that concerns us? If we were to ascend into the realm of the spirit and hear Jesus Christ praying, I believe we would hear something like this:

"Heavenly Father, I am Your Son and I am glorified in Thee. I pray not for Myself, but for My people yet upon the earth, that their faith in Us may not fail, but grow exceedingly. I pray that from their hearts, Our love within them will grow and that Thou would preserve their hearts blameless unto the end. I pray for their knowledge of Us, that they will know that We dwell within them, that We love them exceedingly and care for them. I pray that their joy will remain, that My Word would be exalted within their heart, and that the wicked one would overcome them not with his evil works and wicked devices. I pray that they will know Us in truth within their hearts and that their hearts would be found perfect, pure, clean, and undefiled in Thy sight. I pray that Thou would be unto them their God and they unto Us Our people. Let it be so now. Amen"

Christians continue to seek and search for that which we already have. We daily seek and chase after God in heaven not realizing that God dwells within our hearts. We quickly boast, saying, "I can do all things through Christ," but can Christ do all things through us? We seek the kingdom of God, not realizing that the kingdom of God is within us, and Christ is seated as King upon the throne of our heart. In ignorance, man seeks possessions and wealth above confessions and repentance from his sin. It seems most of us would rather play rather than pray; to receive than give. This has produced a serious negative heart condition in the Body of Christ.

Spiritual heart attacks, strokes, and aneurysms of the brain are rampant because church leadership seeks personal fame and glory. We teach material gain above that of personal holiness. We criticize, socialize, and sit in judgment. We have failed to become the heart specialists and witnesses God requires of us by His written Word. God is not pleased. In leadership, man wants flesh action, but God wants heart action. We seek to fulfill the desires of the flesh, but God is interested in the desires of the heart. Man cannot do God's will from the confines of his flesh. Christianity is heart-operated. We don't know who we are because we're still trying to be what God doesn't want us to be. Satan doesn't care what we do so long as it's not God's will from the heart.

Because of our negligence, the church pews are filled with thousands in serious need of a spiritual heart transplant. If we wish to survive as the church of the Lord Jesus Christ, God must perform an emergency heart operation. We have become comatose in our lifestyle of comfort, sleeping on pillows of praise and worship while our hearts remain far from God. Mark 7:6-8 says, "He answered and said unto them, Well hath Esaias prophesied of you hypocrites, as it is written, This people honoureth me with their lips, but their heart is far from me. Howbeit in vain do they worship me, teaching for doctrines the commandments of men. For laying aside the commandment of God, ye hold the tradition of men, as the washing of pots and cups: and many other such like thing ye do."

This serious matter is a result of our wanting religion more than a relationship with the Lord, desiring to be saved without the presence of the Savior. We hold on to various doctrines and beliefs and have let go of the Master's hands. We look where God doesn't want us to look, which is the outward appearance of the flesh (1 Samuel 16:7). We see what we should not see, think and say what we ought not, and go where angels fear to tread. We have grown out of focus in regard to God's will, plan, and purpose. We want biblical standards to agree with our worldly lifestyle. The Red Sea still flows between man's standards and God's purpose. We must tear down those Jericho walls standing between our prayers to God and the praises of God. We enter into the land of milk and honey to enjoy its fruit but refuse to sow. If there's no change, we'll soon be disconnected from God's presence. It's a serious matter.

Proverbs 23:26 says, "My son, give me thine heart, and let thine eyes observe my ways." Some sincere believers have given their hearts to God, but they have not yet given Him their lives. Other believers have truly given their lives to Christ, but they haven't yet given Him their whole heart. These types of lifestyles will lead to what I've termed as a Code Red condition,which in turn will evolve into a Code Blue state, where cessation of life can be expected.

CODES

According to Webster's dictionary, the term "code" means "a system of principals or rules; or a system of letters, numbers, or symbols used to represent assigned and often secret meanings." There are numerous codes that have been firmly set and well established within this world's system. These are the Morris Code, the Code of Laws, Moral Codes, Codes of Ethics, and Genetic Codes, just to name a few. In order to translate a message sent through codes, you must have the correct decoding program.

There are thousands of key codes, but the most serious and dangerous of all among mankind, the medical profession, and

23

God is Code Blue. When Code Blue is announced in the hospital, controlled chaos breaks out; extreme measures are implemented to prevent the death of a patient. In both the natural and spiritual realms, Code Blue refers to a life or death situation. The Bible is the only decoding book in all the earth that has the answer for a spiritual Code Blue state.

CODE BLUE

Code Blue is a state or event in which the life of the flesh is threatened. If not immediately addressed, death is inevitable. While in this state, professional help is needed right away to pre-vent death. A machine or several instruments may be hooked up to sustain and/or save the person's life. The medical profession has yet to come to the revelation that while they are frantically working to save the natural life of an individual, a spiritual Code Blue state may still be in progress.

The key purpose of this book is to encourage all believers to become more heart-conscious and serious about their faith and salvation and gain the knowledge about situations that lead to Code Red and Code Blue status in our hearts. It is time for us to join together and become more and submit more deeply to God's spiritual heart-care program. It's time for every one of us to become firmly connected with God in our hearts. Our number one priority should be the ability to stand in God's presence with a pure and clean heart. Let us view all things of God as important and serious, not approaching them with a jovial or lighthearted attitude, but rather great concern. In the midst of a dying society, Christ is still our only hope. He will never change, but He will change us into His image by changing our hearts.

I pray that this book will elevate God-consciousness within your mind, bringing forth a clear understanding about the serious conditions and problems of the heart. I pray that many will be made aware of God's position, His mind, and intentions where His people are concerned and that He will uncover any serious heart matter that may hinder our walk with God.

Let us pray:

Dear Heavenly Father, in the precious and matchless name of Jesus, I pray that this book will encourage the Body of Christ to meet your expectation and divine purpose. Keep us from a Code Blue state Lord; cleanse us again. Revive us unto your glory that our designed destiny will be glorious in your presence. Make our hearts right so that favor and virtue may rejoice together and so love from the heart may rule among your people in the earth once again. Increase our faith, Heavenly Father. Code Blue has consumed many hearts and souls, and Code Red is raging out of control. You are our only hope. The only way is truth and life. We need more of you, Lord. Let all who read this book be eternally free from the power, purpose, and presence of both Code Red and Code Blue forever. In Jesus' Name, Amen.

2

CODE BLUE EXPOSED

In the beginning, God formed the first man from the dust of the earth. He was a lifeless mass of dirt without spirit or life. God called Him Adam. Genesis 2:7 reveals that God breathed into Adam's nostrils the "Breath of Life" and he became a living soul. The word "breath" also stands for spirit; therefore, God's "in-breathing" gave Adam's spirit life, and he walked before God in a natural, perfect, sinless body.

God then brought forth beautiful Eve, a helpmate for Adam, formed from a rib taken out of Adam's body, and she became the mother of life. While this was taking place, satan, the author of Code Blue, watched very intently. Eventually, satan waged war against Adam and Eve by poisoning their minds and hearts with lies and deception (Code Blue State). They willingly chose to disobey God's commandments (Code Blue Sin), and died spiritually (Code Blue Dead). Thus "Code Blue State," "Code Blue Sin," and "Code Blue Death" were activated.

From that time until now, every human being born of a woman (except for our Lord) would be inherently evil. From birth, little babies rebel, disobey, and lie without being taught. Genesis 8:21 says, "And the Lord smelled a sweet savour; and the Lord said in his heart, I will not again curse the ground any more for man's sake; for the imaginations of man's heart is evil from his youth." For this reason, we must train our children in the way they should go—the way of the heart. Teaching them the Word, how to be good servants of God, how to worship, pray, and praise God from their heart is of paramount importance. (For additional insight into this truth, study Proverbs 15:11, 17:6;

2 Kings 17:41; Psalm 78:5-8, 89:29-34, and 103:13-17; Jeremiah 2:9-10; Matthew 2:19-23; and Ephesians 6:1-4.)

We enter into a Code Blue State when we don't live by the Word of God. God's Word provides pure, spiritual food and drink for our spirit man. It is the protector of the heart. It's easily digestible and it's full of spiritual nutrients, wealth, health, and strength. The Word of God is a natural deterrent to serious matters of the heart and renders Code Blue powerless. Jesus Christ is the Word of God—the written Word and the spoken Word (John 1:1-14). He overcame Code Red, Code Blue, and serious matters of the heart through the cross of Calvary. However, we must be serious and firm about our faith, conviction, belief, and commitment.

Code Blue is sent and set to ruin, kill, steal, and destroy both the natural and spiritual hearts. Because of this, both hearts require daily protection, much attention, and care. The weapons of Code Blue are sin; transgression of God's laws; rebelliousness; and disobedience against the laws, commandments, and will of God.

Code Blue may present itself as something far beyond your personal ability to understand or control. It gets its power and strength through the elements of surprise and shock. Worry, anger, grief, fear and death follow Code Blue. Sin, rebelliousness, and disobedience lead the way. It loves every negative matter of the heart where pain, sickness, disaster, disease, and death are prone to become a reality. Code Blue stands before God as if to say, "All souls are mine and all will bow down before me with fear and trembling." Without the knowledge of our Christian de-coder—the Bible—this would be the case; however, as we live in Jesus Christ, walk, breathe, and have our being, the Truth makes us free, giving us total victory over all of our Code Blue enemies! By true repentance from the heart, we are delivered from the wiles and tricks of the author of Code Blue, who is satan.

CODE RED

In studying Code Blue, another serious code is brought to light—Code Red. Probably the most common code, it means:

Warning, Caution, Take Notice, Alert, Alarm, Be on the Look-out, SOS, Danger, Risk, Peril, Threat, Jeopardy, Hazard, Menace, Treacherousness, Crisis, M.I.A, Emergency, Vulnerability. In short, Code Red is activated when we hear those "warning bells" in our head. God is speaking to us, warning us of harm when this code is sounded.

Every animal in nature has a Code Red alarm system built within its being. No one has been able to properly identify this built-in warning system other than to call it a survival instinct, a notion, perception, premonition, guess, consciousness, or aware-ness. Whatever you call it, when a Code Red Warning has been issued, it is telling us to do one of three things:

STOP–To halt, pause, stand still, shut down, discontinue, suspend, withdraw, check, cease movement, terminate, quit, fold up, refrain.

LOOK–To view, scan, take a glance, gaze at, stare, inspect, investigate, probe, pry, watch, spy out, observe, examine, give attention to, study, and search out.

LISTEN–To endeavor to hear, be attentive, attend to, keep one's ear open, hearken, heed, take advice, and take into consideration.

This warning device is the voice of God alerting us to immi-nent natural or spiritual danger. His spirit, which encompasses both the natural and the spiritual realms, protects us against the negative serious matters of the heart.

In the spiritual realm, God warns us of Code Red activity by using His audible voice, His written word, a revelation, or a visi-tation to tell us to stop, repent, leave immediately, check our hearts, use our faith, watch, fast and/or pray. When we're faced with a serious matter that has the potential to have a negative effect upon our heart, we know that we're in a Code Red situa-tion. Life is never more serious for anyone than when they are faced with Code Red or Code Blue. It's serious because Code Blue is never far away from Code Red, and both eventually lead to some type of emergency, death, or decay whether it is natural or spiritual.

The difference between Code Red and Code Blue is the fact that Code Blue is a sin unto death and Code Red is a "missing the mark" sin or error against God's Word, will, plan, or purpose. When there is a Code Blue, we know that someone or something, such as a false evil spirit or religion, is trying to kill us or to render us spiritually dead while we are yet fleshly alive.

When we say Code Red, we know that it's a serious emergency that must be addressed immediately. Code Red is always negative to our well-being. In the summer when the heat soars to temperatures of 100 degrees or more and in the winter when the cold plummets to temperatures below zero degrees, a natural Code Red alert is given, especially for those having respiratory problems or heart conditions. Just like Code Blue in its purpose and design, Code Red is no respecter of persons, age, time, or location. When God gives a Code Red warning to the church or to the believer, are we really listening? Do we hear God's Code Red alarm? His warning voice echoes throughout the Body of Christ alerting us to serious heart conditions caused by video games, movie houses, false doctrine, bad TV, not tithing, sin, doubt, and unbelief. It's mandatory that every believer carefully maintain a pure and clean heart so that we hear God's Code Red warning.

The Apostle Paul traveled to Athens, Greece where he beheld the church that had fallen into a Code Red state—one step away from Code Blue. He found them to be very religious; faithfully they made devotions to God, yet God was "the unknown God" (Acts 17:22-23). They worshiped God in ignorance. Yes, they raised their hands to God and some may have given God praise, but their bodies were not God's temple. We must know Him inwardly if our faith is to be sound and firm in Him. Their hearts were not God's dwelling and domain; therefore, Code Red had unchallenged reign. The Apostle Paul began to preach that God gives life and breath to everyone. He preached that God made all things and that all should seek Him, feel after Him, and find Him. For in Him—that is, in Christ Jesus—we all live, move, and have our being. It's time for God's people to take authority over Code Blue and Code Red and let heaven and earth know that we know who our God is.

CODE BLUE NATURAL

Code Blue Natural often strikes without warning. Heart attacks, strokes, high blood pressure, and others often occur due to an undetected, underlying health problem. These things can cause a Code Blue to be issued. When a Code Blue Natural occurs, the essence and quality of life is threatened.

Warning symptoms of an impending Code Blue Natural state are often overlooked. Any circumstances that cause intense pressures or that are committed excessively without restraint are indicators that you are leaving Code Red and entering into a Code Blue state. Bad food, defiled water, unclean air, same-sex marriages, Godless societies, and the defying of God's moral codes that sustains human life are serious pitfalls that leads to code blue.

CODE BLUE SPIRITUAL

In this state, the Christian exists without acknowledging the presence of God. Their spiritual life is in "grave" danger. The breath of God within their spirit man, the hidden man of the heart (1 Peter 3:4), has almost stopped—they have religion without a relationship, they pray, not knowing His promises, and they praise and worship without a right heart. Thirty-minute prayers and two-hour church services are too much. They worship and pray on Sunday only and read God's Word only every now and then. Sin is acceptable and almost seems necessary.

THREE MAJOR COMPONENETS OF CODE BLUE SPIRITUAL

The three major components of Code Blue Spiritual, which are initiated by serious matters of the heart are:

Code Blue State: Trial, Trouble, Warfare, Sickness, and Disease

Code Blue Sin: Bondage, Rebelliousness, Disobedience, Backsliding, Unbelief, and Darkness

Code Blue Death: Lifeless, Darkness, without a relationship with God–Spiritually Dead

CODE BLUE STATE

A survey, conducted on Christian radio and television, recently found that more than 30,000 pastors, teachers, and church members worldwide left the local assembly, never to return. Something overwhelmed their hearts, spread through their minds, wills, souls and emotions, cutting off the breath of God. In John 20:22, Christ breathed upon His disciples the Holy Ghost, thus imparting additional heart protection into their spirit. Whatever crisis should arise, they now had inner heart-strength to survive. (See Acts 17:24-28.)

Administering Code Blue in this earthly realm are many demons and death angels. All anti-God systems that exist are married to Code Blue and cannot be separated, destroyed, or eliminated by mankind until the return of Jesus Christ. A Code Blue State evolves quickly in a believer's life when they sin and won't repent or they try to live a double lifestyle. Some experience Code Blue when they try to serve God from the mind and not the heart. Code Blue manifests when we confess to be holy, saved, and born again but haven't completely given our hearts to Jesus Christ. Every heart upon the earth that is void of the presence of God is a prime candidate and potential dwelling place for Code Blue. For some, a Code Blue experience is a result of error in interpreting scripture, lack of proper information, false doctrine, walking in the flesh, ignorance, rebelliousness, disobedience, sin, evil thoughts, wicked imaginations, etc. If these seeds are allowed to grow, the harvest will be disaster, crisis, sickness, disease, or–worst of all–separation from the will of God and removal from His presence.

CODE BLUE SIN

In a Code Blue state, serious problems, such as spiritual attacks, inward wicked thoughts and imaginations, ignorance, and unholy reverence toward God and His word, have damaged and weakened the believer's relationship with God. Spiritual Code Blue patients are also those in Christ who, by personal choice, still live a double lifestyle, have no real prayer life, walk by sight and not by faith, love only those who love them, and hear the Word each Sunday but whose hearts are hardened by the lust of the flesh, lust of the eyes, and the pride of life. The serious spiritual matter of Code Blue sin occurs as the Christian turns away from God and allows doubt, unbelief, and sin to clog their spiritual arteries. This posture hinders the flow of God's anointing throughout the body of our spirit man. A consistent, flesh-pleasing lifestyle may activate a spiritual stroke or a serious heart attack. These Christians may continue to go to church each Sunday but are not aware that Spiritual Code Blue has attacked them. There is a diminishing desire to walk with Christ; the will to seek and serve Him is gone. The prime purpose, plan, and power of Code Blue is to kill the believer's desire to excel in God. It never says no to sin and death.

CODE BLUE DEATH

In Proverbs 4:23, we see that out of our heart flow the issues of life. In Proverb 23:7 we learn that as a man thinketh in his heart, so is he, and in Romans 10:10a, we read, "For with the heart man believeth unto righteousness." Unfortunately, the Church has erred in that it has not yet identified the heart as the greatest power of concern in our daily lives as God and medical doctors all over the world do in every Code Blue or Code Red situation. The first thing a medical doctor does to a Code Blue victim, even before any life saving medication is given, is to check their heart. The heart monitor or pulse is checked to determine the strength of the patient's life signals. Our Great Heart Physician (Jesus Christ) does the same thing when we present our bodies, with seriousness; infrastructure problems either natural or spiritual; He checks our heart's condition to see if there is enough faith and love for complete recovery. He knows that every Code Blue circumstance or situation can be countered by heart recon- struction and cleansing. Heart cleansing in God's presence is sec- ond only to salvation. Man looks upon faith to increase in riches or personal benefits, while God uses faith to purify the heart. Acts 15:8-9 says, "And God, which knoweth the hearts, bare them wit- ness, giving them the Holy Ghost, even as he did unto us; And put no difference between us and them, purifying their hearts by faith." Truly man looks on the outward appearance and fails, but God looks on the heart and wins (1 Samuel 16:7). Code Blue is every dead or unclean thing. All things that cannot produce life are directly linked to Code Blue. The more we die to self and sin- ful flesh, the more we come alive in Christ. The more we put to death all anti-God concepts—such as iniquities, transgressions, and disobedience—the less power any dead thing will have in our lives. Dead and unclean things are often resurrected back into our lives by the desires, motives, intents, and thoughts of our mind and heart.

Code Blue death is the most serious matter of the heart. It eliminates God consciousness, rendering all as lifeless, useless, motionless, and inactive. Code Blue Death causes all to walk as if dead to God's will, purpose, power, and eternal word for life. This Code Blue State has created a large group of people in the Body of Christ whom I call the "church chasers." These are hear- ers and not doers of the Word. These enter into a church assem- bly looking for the exit signs and keeping track of the clock. They confess Christ, but they do not truly possess Him. To confess and not possess is a very serious matter of the heart. Even we who are Bible addicts, church praisers, worshipers, and prayer addicts are sometimes deceived because we think that an event of Code Blue could never happen to us. This is not so.

Even if we love the Lord with all of our hearts, the Scriptures command that we also love one another as we love God and our- selves. Matthew 5:22-23 teaches us that God doesn't want us to come into His presence with gifts if we have anything against our brother (neighbor). Why? Love is a great antidote against serious matters of the heart and against Code Blue. Love adds years to the natural body and eternal blessings to the spiritual body. While church clergy argue and separate over issues such as doctrine, high titles, and women in ministry, God is focused upon the heart and its immediate need for protection against Code Blue. We, the church, must be revived in areas of our hearts if we expect to survive the power and attacks of Code Blue. For it is not just what we take with us as we leave this world and ascend to glory, but also what we leave behind.

CODE BLUE CASES—REAL LIFE TESTIMONIES

CODE BLUE CASE #1

NAME: RANDY DOWNING

This is the true story of Randy Downing, my nephew, whose physical condition at birth had thrust him into war with Code Blue Natural for over 40 years. Doctors at Coffeyville Kansas Medical diagnosed Randy with sickle cell anemia. Sickle cell anemia is a diseased condition of blood cells that inhibits oxygen and nutrients from being properly distributed throughout the body, causing great pain within the joints and muscles throughout the entire body. Many African-Americans and a few Caucasian have this trait. However, when both father and mother have the trait, the chances are greater that the children will be affected.

Both of Randy's parents had the trait, and he was the first of five born with this dreadful, life-threatening disease. The family was shocked when the doctors pronounced a death sentence on Randy—he would die by the age of five. Code Blue Natural had staked a claim on Randy's life. Nevertheless, Randy had parents of faith who knew how to pray. As Randy approached the age of five, his parents spent many sleepless nights in prayer for him unto God. His fifth birthday came and went. The doctors admitted that he was truly a miracle child. However, they were certain he wouldn't live to see the age of ten.

Randy enrolled in school, played ball, learned how to fish, and worked hard with his parents. His parents believed God and kept hope alive with faithful hearts. Randy's miracle continued to manifest. His parents placed Randy's Code Blue Natural state upon the altar of God's grace and mercy through faith. He experienced many sickle cell crises in which over 150 blood transfusions were required. At times the pain in his body often more than he could bear. At the age of eight, Randy gave his life to Christ. On his tenth birthday his doctors scratched their heads and looked upon him in awe, for Code Blue Natural had been held in check through prayer and faith in God. Again, these doctors, not realizing that they were witnesses to a miracle, pronounced yet another death sentence on Randy—the unbelieving doctors stated firmly that he would never live to be 21.

Even after 100 lifesaving operations, Code Blue Natural wasn't going to give up or allow Randy any real joy and peace. But through it all, Randy found joy and peace when he began to walk closely with Christ at the young age of 15. By this time, he was officially labeled as a medical miracle. With over 175 emergency room visits to his record, at the age of 21, the doctors confessed that the God of Randy Downing is truly a keeper and a life-preserving God, but surely 30 years of age had to be Randy's maximum life expectancy. There had been no other case in the history of that hospital where one born with the disease had lived for so long.

Code Blue Natural changed tactics and attacked Randy's younger sister, Karen, who had a stroke and died. Then it was discovered that his younger brother, John, aged 16, also had the disease. This was impossible, the doctors exclaimed, for sickle cell anemia is a birth disease only! Not so in the case of John Downing. Within a few years, John passed away. Through it all, Randy held on to his faith in God. The agony, frustration, and grief of the Downing family were greatly magnified beyond words, but their faith in God never changed. Randy enrolled in medical school and, after eight years of study, crisis after crisis, many blood transfusions, and countless sleepless, pain-filled nights, Randy graduated from medical college with a degree in pharmacy.

Today, at the age of 40, Randy works at a Pharmaceutical Lab when he's able. At times he admits himself into the hospital for special treatment to preserve his natural life. He loves the Lord, and Jesus Christ is his daily confession. He will tell you that to God alone be the glory. As I write this story, Randy has been to funerals of many of his aunts, uncles, and close friends. Recently, his father was diagnosed with cancer. When I called Randy to get his permission to write his story, I asked him how he survived this great test. He said, "Uncle Don, I learned at a young age how to forget about what happened last year, last month, and yesterday and put my trust in God for all of my tomorrows." Each day that Randy lives is a serious matter of the heart.

CODE BLUE CASE #2

NAME: MR. COLUMBUS GAMBRELL

I first met Mr. and Mrs. Gambrell when they hired me to do some home improvement work on their home. During my time in their home, I spoke to Mrs. Gambrell–Claudia–about being saved according to scripture. I believe at that time she had a head-knowledge of salvation, like many people in her denomination, but that knowledge did not extend to the heart. Approximately one year had passed when she called me saying, "Pastor Downing, I'm coming to your church to receive the Holy Spirit just like the Bible says–I'm not sure about my salvation." True to her word, she came one Sunday with her daughter, and God filled both of them with the precious gift of the Holy Spirit. Later in the service, she testified that the doctors had discovered cancer in her body; there was little hope. Code Blue Natural had struck again. The next month she was baptized, along with her husband, Claudius Gambrell, and her daughter.

Approximately two years later, on July 15, 1997, Mrs. Claudia Gambrell succumbed to cancer and passed away to her destiny. It was a sad day for every heart. We had been an established church for over ten years, and this was the very first funeral of any church member or relative of Heart To Heart Christian Center.

On September 4, 1998, Claudius went to his physician for his annual health check up. To his amazement, he was also stricken by Code Blue Natural demon of cancer. With tears in his eyes, his friend and personal doctor looked at him and told him that his life expectancy was no more than two or three weeks. His cancer count (P.S.A. test) was over 1500. He immediately went into the hospital to get a second opinion. He refused to believe the first report. The second opinion from the hospital reported that he might live for up to two months. He boldly told the presiding doctors and nurses that he was a child of God and that he was not going to die. He said that he wasn't ready and that, in the name of Jesus, they were wrong. The war was on. Fate stood up against destiny. Code Blue declared war on mercy. Death and disease went to battle with health and wholeness. Code Blue dispatched fear and worry upon his heart, but Mr. Gambrell held on to his confession. Even when he went to the bathroom and nothing came forth but blood, he still said, "No" to Code Blue.

He came one Sunday to Heart to Heart Christian Center and together we prayed the prayer of faith. We gave him biblical scriptures to increase his faith. (In his 45 years of going to church, he had never been a Bible student.) He obeyed our instructions. He believed and God responded. To the utter amazement of his doctors, his P.S.A. count began to recede as he stood on God's word.

This is the full documented account.

• October 22, 1998, P.S.A. count 950.

• November 4, 1998, P.S.A. count 790.

• March 8, 1999, P.S.A. count 352.6.

• April 15, 1999, P.S.A. count 342.7.

On May 5, 1999, he came again to Heart To Heart Christian Center with a smile on his face and a voice full of faith for his cancer's P.S.A count had declined from 1500 to 66.5. We laid our hands upon him believing with him for total victory.

- May 19, 1999, P.S.A. count 59.

- June 17, 1999, P.S.A. count 38.3.

- July 31, 1999, P.S.A. count 26.7.

- August 20, 1999, P.S.A. count 11.4.

- September 1999, P.S.A. count 10.7.

- October 1999, P.S.A. count 5.6.

- In November of 1999, his P.S.A. count had declined to 5.4, and the doctors said that there was no need for him to come to have the tests done so often.

- In February 2001, his P.S.A. count was .01.

- On May 1, 2001, I saw him in the church giving God the highest praise, for there was no detection of cancer at all. His P.S.A. count was 00.001. Code Blue was totally defeated.

Today Mr. Gambrell is a man full of faith who travels to local cancer centers and churches giving his miracle testimony. They call him the miracle man, but he demands that all glory be given to God above. He takes each day seriously and keeps my first book, *Hidden Treasures of the Heart*, always close by.

CODE BLUE #3—A SAVED HEART

NAME: PORCIA A. HARDY

NARRATED BY: MRS. PORCIA HARDY, JUNE 15, 2001

I was married and saved when I encountered my first Code Blue State. I worked for a corporation that required my team to inspect areas under construction, ensuring that the vendors were providing the requested services and building materials. I entered a building area that was in its final stages of completion–the painting had just been completed and the carpet laid. While inspecting the area, my breath was taken away, and I began to hold my chest. As I exited the area, another employee noticed I was gasping for breath and asked the front desk to call the paramedics. When the paramedics arrived, they checked my heart and oxygen levels. The vice president requested that I be taken to the hospital; however, I wanted to go to a hospital closer to home and went later on that evening. I was admitted that night. I had an allergic reaction to the fumes from the carpet glue. Code Blue State was trying to take me over.

The worst part was being taken from Fort Washington Hospital to Washington Hospital Center where they did several tests. One of them was a cardiac catheterization, checking for blocked arteries. While I waited, I heard a Code Blue warning over the PA system for another patient. I had an anxiety attack. I was a nervous wreck. I could hardly breathe. I felt as if I would die. They had to calm me down by putting nitroglycerin under my tongue. Code Blue was really trying to grip me. The doctors finally proceeded with the cauterization after my elevated blood pressure—caused by panic about the situation—was stable. After they performed the cardiac catheterization, I was hysterical. It felt as if an elephant was sitting on my chest. I kept screaming and crying out about the pain. The nurses kept checking my vital signs and could not figure out what was going on. They monitored me all afternoon. The next day, they found out that I was allergic to the iodine that was used to run through my blood stream in order to do the catheterization test. I was told that people who were allergic to this type of iodine or similar allergies have died because they did not know they were allergic to iodine medication. This was the first time I found out that I was allergic to iodine. I thank God I was saved because this could have been my last story.

I am a woman who has been through several tests of faith. I have lived through seven previous major surgeries. The seventh was the ultimate test of faith to me. In January 1999, I went in for a simple physical. I had no symptoms, no pain, just a little growth in my mouth that I thought was allergy related. I was diagnosed

40

with cancer of the mouth! My ENT specialist was shocked to find a person with cancer in the mouth that had never smoked or chewed tobacco. When the doctor told me that the biopsy was cancerous, I said to myself, "Oh my God, I am by myself." God spoke to me right in her office and said, "I'm with you, I will never leave you or forsake you." The doctor asked me if I was okay. I said, "Yes," but I was trying to listen to her and God at the same time. Then that little voice said, "I'm going to use you to bring your family together. Starting with you, today, ask your family members to forgive everything that has happened in the family from 1998 on back." While God was speaking to me, the doctor was asking me if I was okay.

Little did I know it was just the beginning. My battle would turn into a war with Code Blue. I had to make arrangements immediately to have the cancer removed. In my mind, doubt and unbelief warred with faith and trust. God's word became harder to encompass in my vocabulary. Dr. Martinez told me she did not know how long the cancer had been there and whether it had spread. She also explained to me that I would never be the same again. She gave me the worst-case scenario and told me I would have to learn how to eat and talk all over again. Being saved and anointed helped during the radiation treatments on my face and mouth, but it was still horrible.

There were times I could not talk, eat, or drink. I lost 20 pounds. My radiologist, Dr. Simmons, said it was amazing because my blood count never changed during the 30 treatments of radiation. The next week, I agreed to have surgery. The cancer I had was a type of cancer that could travel to other parts of my body, so they took me through several tests—a mammogram, an ultrasound, a bone scan, and a CT scan. While I waited to hear the results, which took a total of 2 months, sleep flooded me and fear and hurt rested upon my heart as I thought about the unknown. Each test was taken at different times, and the results were coming in at different times—they weren't positive.

While waiting, I thanked God for my salvation, for in my trials, right in the midst of Code Blue, I learned to put on the whole armor of God. My husband and I read the Word together every morning; we were of one accord in everything we did. I fed my spirit morning, noon, night, and in between. The more I worshiped and praised God, the more He sent me various signs of his mighty-working power. One time when I was alone praying, God's still voice said, "*What does the Bible say about being sick?*" I replied, "If there is any sick among you go to the elders of the church." So all day I asked my husband, sisters, and anyone who called if they knew of a revival going on. There was just one. I went there and got prayer. I obeyed the Word of God.

That next morning, God woke me up at 2:38 a.m. It was so amazing because immediately I was wide awake. He spoke to me and said, "*I want you to **believe** that when the preacher and evangelist prayed for you that you were completely healed. When you get the confirmation from the medical doctors, I want you to go back to that church and tell it.*" A chill came over my body and I just cried and cried with tears of joy. I couldn't wait until the alarm clock went off to tell my husband. The next night God woke me up again and said in the quiet still voice, "*Now that I have taken care of you, I want you to be an intercessor.*" I immediately began to intercede in prayer for everyone I could think of. The Great Physician had spoken. I heard Him and believed. But Code Blue had not departed, for I had to learn how to walk by faith in the midst of the storm.

When I got the results back from my CT scan, the oncologist saw four spots on my liver. My doctor and the Oncologist said they knew two were cancerous cells, but they not sure about the other two. My distraught husband almost passed out. I sat quiet and still. I was waiting to hear from God, but at this time He said nothing. God doesn't ever have to repeat himself, for all of His works were finished from the foundation of the world (Hebrew 4:3). I asked the oncologist if I could have chemotherapy, but she said that it would do no good. I then asked about radiation. She said, "No, because that would cook the liver." My husband and I left the office devastated and without any hope. Slowly, we drove home; both of us were quiet in the car. I even took the long way home because I wanted to meditate and clear my heart. As soon as my husband and I got in the house, we took our family Bible, fell to our knees, and began to pray. I prayed out loud, binding Code Blue and the spirits of darkness. I said, "The doctors can do nothing, but Jesus, You are my doctor, and I'm going to put all my trust in you."

From that day forward it was a serious, heated battle. I had to go back in my mind and remember what God had told me that early morning—to believe that I was healed. I had to tell myself that God does not do anything half way. If he told me I was healed then I had to believe that I was healed. He would heal not only my mouth, but my liver, too. My husband and I decided that we would continue to be of one accord, praying and reading certain scriptures every morning until I got my final tests. I even told my doctor that I wanted the CT Scan of my liver to be done again because of what God had told me.

During this time, I received a confirmation from a friend who was a member of Ebenezer AME church. He called us one Sunday to tell us that the pastor, Rev. Browning, had said, "There is someone in this congregation who has a good friend that has cancer of the mouth. Tell her she is healed." This was before the CT scan was re-done. The equipment broke down, which caused me to wait longer. The agony of waiting was taking a toll on my husband—he knew there was nothing he could do but pray. Multitudes of prayers were prayed on my behalf. Friends of friends, coworkers, my church family, and others were sending up many prayers. Finally, almost six months after my surgery, another scan was taken and I was called while at work with the good news. Code Blue was defeated! A year later, in 2001, my doctor admitted the following: "I honestly didn't know which way your case was going to go; you made a believer out of me, and I am glad to be a part of your godly miracle." Later he revealed to me that less than five percent of the people who have mouth and liver cancer of my type survive. As a humble child, I now strive to learn more and more of Him and His Word daily. Today, I look at life in a totally different way and praise God more and more everyday. God gets all the glory. I was just a chosen vessel. By God's mighty, miracle-working power, Code Blue Natural lost the battle once again. Bishop Downing's book, *Hidden Treasure Of The Heart*, stays by my bedside. I read it as a reminder to keep my heart spiritually serious, because in my research of my type of cancer less than 5% of the patients who are victims of my type of cancer ever survive.

CODE BLUE CASE #4—A NEW HEART

NAME: BARBARA MAE WILLIAMS

This is the story of my very own mother-in-law, who wasn't saved and had a serious alcohol addiction. She was stricken by a Code Blue State, which caused both of her kidneys to fail. Immediately, Code Blue rushed in as a flood and swallowed her whole; she fell into a deep coma. The family of believers began to pray fervently for her salvation, deliverance, and healing. The doctors called for last rites. It was a serious matter of the heart, a situation in which Code Blue Natural had claimed total victory. I went to her bedside under the anointing power of God; I approached her praying in the Spirit. She was lying there, motionless, as if dead. I reached out to touch her; she quickly tried to get away from me even though she was in a deep coma, at the point of death. I tried to touch her three times with the same response. The Holy Spirit spoke from within my heart saying, "*Don, don't you recognize that a demon spirit has consumed her? You must remember that whatever you bind on earth shall be bound in heaven, and whatsoever you loose on earth, I will loose in heaven.*" With boldness, I ministered unto her calling upon the name of the Lord Jesus Christ.

She continued to try to avoid me as Code Blue began to digest her life. The death angel was sent to her beside, fully prepared to complete its work. I left the hospital with a heart full of concern. Unknown to me, my wife and her praying aunts and cousins were on their way. As they entered the hospital, the doctor stated that she was clinically dead. Code Blue had apparently won. They all began to petition the Lord, fervently binding and loosing with tears and much faith. Five minutes went by. The nurses and doctors were around her bedside. Seven minutes passed and there were no life functions. It was over. The doctors had done all that they could. But, after eight minutes, just when they were about to unplug all of the life support equipment Barbara Mae Williams came back to life!

Her testimony tells of her entering a great white room where the Spirit of God spoke to her from a huge wide bed saying you must go back, now is not the time. As she turned away and walked back down a long ladder, she found herself back in her body with her eyes open wide. Today she is the church secretary—saved, sanctified, and filled with the Holy Spirit.

CODE BLUE CASE #5

FAITHLESS HEARTS FOUND IN MARK 4:35-41

Jesus Christ was a boat with His disciple when unexpectedly there arose a great wind, and water began to fill the boat—the boat was sinking. Code Blue had arrived. Death was only a few moments away. The scripture states that Jesus was asleep on the stern or back of the boat upon a pillow. Although Jesus' flesh was asleep, I believe His spirit never slept, just as God never sleeps. I believe that the Holy Spirit kept Christ's body in a sleeping state so that God could sow more faith deeper into the faithless hearts of His disciples. After the disciples awakened Jesus, He said to Code Blue, "Peace, be still!" Code Blue immediately ceased its purpose, plan, and power. Death left the scene and waited for another day, and the demons went back to their master, satan, in total defeat. Jesus turned to His disciples and questioned them, knowing their hearts still lacked the faith required for total victory. "Why are you so fearful? How is it that you have no faith?" Jesus asked.

What this means to us is that we must use the kind of faith that God gives to us so that we can defeat the wiles, tricks, and even the death sentence of Code Blue. We must keep a positive attitude of heart and discard the negative, faithless, useless heart of fear, doubt, and unbelief. Had Jesus believed the same as His disciples and spoken the same negative words they spoke– "we perish"–Code Blue would have destroyed the boat and all of the men in it. The boat was full of water and was beginning to sink; deadly circumstances had risen beyond the disciple's power, throwing them all into a temporary season of defeat. Yet, God knows what to do when circumstances override our faith. He's still saying to Code Blue, "Peace, be still!" but few today have the ears to hear. We're still living in the sinking boat of this dead society. It's like we have a sleeping Jesus in the back seat of our expensive automobiles that are headed for a Code Blue crash. It's time for us to tell Code Blue "Peace, be still."

Peace always has the power to make Code Blue be still. In other words, we must speak positive words of faith and command Code Blue to stop its deadly attitude and evil purpose. Then there will be great calm. Jesus looked upon His disciples, asking them, "Why were you fearful of Code Blue? Why were you negative when a positive statement of faith-filled words was mandatory for your survival? Don't you know that–even though I am with you–victory never manifests itself where a negative, faithless heart rules?"

The lesson is this: we must have faith in God and never doubt Him. When serious matters of the heart manifest in our lives, we need to put the spiritual muzzle of faith over our mouths to stop our hearts from speaking faithless, destructive words. Proverbs 6:2 says, "Thou art snared with the words of thy mouth; thou art taken with the words of thy mouth." Proverbs 30:32 expounds, "If thou hast been foolish in lifting thyself up, or if thou hast thought evil, lay thine hand upon thy mouth." Matthew 12:34 says, "O generation of vipers, how can ye, being evil, speak good things? for out of the abundance of the heart the mouth speaketh." (For more on this subject, see: Job 15:56; Psalm 39:1; Proverbs 16:23, 26:28; Isaiah 29:13; and Colossians 3:8.)

There are many other cases of Code Blue and many serious matters of the heart found within the pages of the Bible. One is chronicled in Genesis after the fall of Adam and Eve. Their two sons, Cain and Abel, were two of the first people embroiled in a Code Blue State. Abel had a righteous heart; Cain had a wicked heart. One day, Cain became incensed with jealousy and killed his brother Abel (Genesis 4:8-15). While the scripture doesn't tell us about the grief, hurt, and anguish that Adam and Eve must have felt upon hearing about their son's death at the hand of their other son, we can imagine their pain. Code Blue was manifested and grew as the earth's population grew. Soon, the earth was full of people with evil hearts. God, who knows every heart, brought forth a great flood, destroying all living things except Noah and his family (Genesis 6: 5-7 and 7:1-24). Noah and his family replenished the earth, but it wasn't long before Code Blue sin was once again rampant on the earth. Sodom and Gomorrah, two notoriously evil cities, were destroyed by God as a result of the widespread Code Blue Sin in the hearts of their people (Genesis 19:15-29).

In the present day, it is obvious that Code Blue Sin is still manifesting itself throughout the earth. Eventually, each person on earth will have to answer for the status of his or her own heart. Here in America, there has been a steady decline of people's interest in the things of God. However, a tragic event seems to have brought some positive results, as people seem to be examining their hearts in relation to God once again. That event, of course, was September 11, 2001.

SEPTEMBER 11, 2001

God had a message for each one of us in the September 11th disaster. We need to search our hearts, get our house in order, and be ready for Jesus to return. God wants all Americans and people of concern to look at their hearts. He wants to be pleased with the heart of America. God leaves no stones unturned when it comes to getting a message to His people.

God prepares the heart of his children for any disaster that may take place. How do I know? For the last six months there has been a great "move of God"—a manifestation of His presence and magnificent power—in every church in which I have ministered. I know now that it was God's preparation. While it is commonly believed that September 11th was an attack on America, I believe that it was first and foremost an attack on the God in whom America trusts and serves. Things don't just happen without cause.

Did God see this coming? How could God allow this to happen? Is this going to continue? These are just a few of the questions that came into the minds of all Americans on that fateful day. Of course God knew it was going to happen. He is omniscient. Of course he allowed disaster, bombing, and death. And yes, it may well happen again and again if America and the entire world do not turn from their wicked ways and repent.

God allows all things to happen for a purpose or for His purpose, and the Scriptures must be fulfilled. Matthew 24:6 says, "And ye shall hear of wars and rumours of wars: see that ye be not troubled: for all these things must come to pass, but the end is not yet." All things do work together for the good of those who love the Lord—the Scriptures cannot be broken. Romans 8:28 promises, "And we know that all things work together for good to them that love God, to them who are the called according to his purpose."

It's time for America to admit that we do not know it all and to turn from following and bowing down to other nations. We desperately need God to lead and guide us once again, to restore us, love us, and bring us back to the nation that we once were. We know that He hears every nation that prays and obeys the Lord Jesus Christ. Proverbs 16:18 tells us that pride goes before destruction and that a haughty spirit (heart) goes before a fall. I believe that the soaring abortion rate, same sex marriages, and the high divorce rate among Christians, are a setup for Code Blue.

Because of the attacks on America, we saw both sinner and saint fall down upon their knees on national television. In the schools, children and teachers prayed together. Six presidents came together in Washington, D.C. for prayer, while congressmen and senators stood in front of the capitol building to pray. The racists set aside their racism and prejudice—no one cared about another's gender or race when the attack took place. All worked side by side, eating, sleeping, and working together as one body. There were no lower or higher class citizens. In this way, God showed that He still breathes life into dead situations.

BE ENCOURAGED; GOD IS NOT MOCKED

The first attack on the World Trade Centers in 1996 was not successful enough to awaken America. It was not recognized as a Code Red warning. So the terrorist nations, with their morbid, evil, black hearts, came together again with a plan to hijack airplanes and fly suicide missions in the power of Code Blue. Their focus was on the Pentagon, the World Trade Centers, the White House, and Camp David. While some of America still slept, they came, crashing two jetliners into America's pride, the twin towers of the World Trade Center. After two commercial jetliners—with more than 150 people and 10 terrorists on each plane—crashed into the towers, thousands of people from every nation, working together inside the twin towers, lost their lives. During the same hour, another plane, carrying more than 100 passengers and six terrorists, crashed into the largest military defense complex in the world, the Pentagon. Code Blue was at its best. It was killing, stealing, and destroying as it was designed by satan to do.

Hundreds within the Pentagon lost their lives in Code Blue. Meanwhile, another flight carrying several terrorists was headed for Camp David to crash into it, but the people on that airplane rose up against them and the military shot the plane down.

The element of surprise has always been satan's prime weapon. In New York thousands of body parts were blown over a 10-block radius. It was one of the worst crime scenes in history. The result of the terrorist attacks was no more than atrocities of

49

Code Blue. Code Blue was victorious, yet God was not mocked. All of a sudden America awoke—stunned, shocked, and hurting and came together as one nation under God. It stood upon its mighty feet and began to pray to the God of heaven.

On September 11th, no one was interested in the Jerry Springer show, the soaps, or the latest hit movie or song. The Word of God came forth against Code Blue, alive and well and full of power. Pastors across the country called on believers to obey 2 Chronicles 7:14-15, which says, "If my people, which are called by my name, shall humble themselves, and pray, and seek my face, and turn from their wicked ways; then will I hear from heaven, and will forgive their sin, and will heal their land."

America had been held as a prisoner in the cells of its own power, separated from God. Just like Paul and Silas were thrown into a Roman jail and began to sing and pray, America turned to God with eyes wide open. God was and is not mocked. The events of September 11, 2001 caused America to return to God. Psalm 3:5-6 says, "I laid me down and slept; I awaked; for the Lord sustained me. I will not be afraid of ten thousands of people, that have set themselves against me round about." (See Isaiah 51:7-9 for more about this concept.)

Christ was the precious balm that America poured on its wounds of pain and grief after the disaster of September 11, 2001. If we are to survive, we must pray that prayer and the gospel of Jesus Christ return to the songs of this nation, that reverence for the Word of God return to the business and political worlds, and that people all over this nation turn from false religions. God is not mocked! It is God's mighty power, not our military strength, that will determine America's future. No longer can it be God bless America, but America bless God! The heart is the key to our success or defeat.

The heart will always gravitate to its surroundings. It will adjust itself continually to whatever it is confronted with, especially what we see, say, hear, and think. The heart of every terrorist is lost. Their minds are sick from the many years of brainwashing; their emotions are unbalanced and in need of the true Lord and Savior.

Terrorists live daily in a state of Code Blue because of their own hearts and minds. Their hearts are made evil from their youth (Genesis 8:21). God brought America back together in unity and oneness of mind, but He is not finished with her yet. He's preparing to return soon, but there is yet another season to go through and another hill to climb.

Man is not in control of his tomorrows. God alone ultimately determines man's destiny. It's time for America to focus again upon the will of God; we must look at what God is doing and desire to act through His power. America as a nation under God must obey God, be cleansed of her sins, and obey God's voice. Each time Code Blue attacks, the Body of Christ must search its heart and God's Word to hear what God is saying, doing and wants to do. Through repentance and forgiveness, America can gain the victory over Code Blue.

America must return to the very God who made her beautiful. No longer should we hold money as more valuable than the lives and the souls of our citizens. In past years, money has grown to be the god of America, and this must not continue. Love is greater than money, and the value of salvation far exceeds that of houses and lands. We must let God be God. God is not mocked; whatever we sow we will also reap. Now is the time for America to remember God, turn from wickedness, and seek the Lord with all her heart. We must renew our strength in God's Word with prayer and true holiness. Let us humble ourselves under His mighty hands and focus upon the condition of the heart of this country, for we have all sinned and come far short of the glory of God (Romans 3:23). We must all confess the Great Heart Physician, the Lord Jesus Christ, if we are to survive as a nation undivided and indivisible under God.

Let the president say that Jesus Christ is Lord. Let congress, the Senate and all of this nation's leaders—regardless of culture—confess the Lord Jesus Christ. Let all citizens of this nation confess the Lord Jesus Christ so that all can experience true freedom. Fear is at war with freedom. While we have been as Simon the Sorcerer, filled with witchcraft, let us repent and heed the voice of the apostle Peter. Acts 8:20-22 says, "But Peter said unto him, Thy money perish with thee, because thou hast thought that the gift of God may be purchased with money. Thou hast neither part nor lot in this matter: for thy heart is not right in the sight of God. Repent therefore of this thy wickedness, and pray God, if perhaps the thought of thine heart may be forgiven thee."

Let it be known unto all that the greatest enemy America faces is not terrorists, China, the economy, or death. The greatest enemy we face today is in the spirit realm, the heart, and in churches that hold to false doctrines and non-biblical concepts. This is why judgment must first begin (and has now begun) in the house of God. 1 Peter 4:17 says, "For the time is come that judgment must begin at the house of God: and if it first begins at us, what shall the end be of them that obey not the gospel of God?"

Millions have already perished, are perishing, and will perish as a result of false religion. They come forth every Sunday to worship in buildings without God's presence; they praise God without having a personal, intimate relationship with Him. Be warned, but yet be encouraged, for whatsoever we sow, that will be the very thing that we will harvest.

3

THE CONTENTS AND INTENTS OF THE HEART

It was a beautiful day, the temperature was a lovely 75 degrees, and I had been praising God at every stoplight, a personal habit of mine. I saw in the distance a 7-11 convenience store, pulled my automobile into its parking lot, and went inside. I got a cold juice drink and stood in line behind a lady who was buying several packs of cigarettes. All of a sudden a pack of cigarettes fell to the floor and, being a gentleman, I stooped down to get the cigarettes for her. I noticed the warning from the surgeon general of the United States, which read, "Warning! The contents of this product causes cancer."

Who in their right mind would smoke one of these?" I thought to myself. It's suicide!" I must have spoken out loud because the lady looked at me with a hopeless, despondent countenance and said, "Sir, I would love to stop smoking, but I just can't. I've tried everything, but nothing has worked for me." With a look of disgust, she left the store. I paid for my juice drink and walked out behind her. "I wonder if she's saved," I thought. She seemed to be such a pleasant and nice lady. "Why are so many people bound by things detrimental to their health and well-being?" I asked the Lord. The Lord spoke in my spirit saying, *"My son, they are not fully aware of the contents and intents. There are those who know the contents of the natural and yet don't realize that there are also contents of the spiritual. Both the contents and intents of the spiritual determine the condition of the heart. Why didn't you tell her?"* I asked the Lord to please forgive me for not being a witness for Him. Mark 7:18-20 came into my mind, which says, "And he saith unto them, Are ye so without understanding also? Do ye not perceive, that whatsoever thing from without entereth into the man, it cannot defile him; Because it entereth not into his heart, but into the belly, and goeth out into the draught, purging all meats? And he said, That which cometh out of the man, that defileth the man."

Webster's New World Thesaurus defines the word "intents" to mean "purpose, aim, determination, and plans [of the heart]" and "contents" to mean "ingredient, the matter contained, it's components, elements, subject matter, and substance." Thus, all that our hearts contain is the sum total of who we really are. We live and speak by the contents of our hearts. What our hearts contain seeks to assert its power to operate in and through us. Is that something beneficial or detrimental to our walk with God? A complete heart inspection is mandatory in order to answer this question. Heart wars are raging—Code Blue Death has destroyed many souls because the people were unaware of the hidden desires of their hearts. Jesus Christ came from the contents of God's heart for the sole purpose of dwelling in the hearts of man. Therefore, when God views our heart, He expects to see His Son there. Satan's ultimate desire is also to fill our hearts and rule from within, controlling our thoughts, imaginations, and actions.

Our hearts are the foundation for our lives and God's ultimate focus. For years, we have been taught to look upon sin, to war, struggle, rebuke, and fight sin, when we should have been taught to focus where God is focused—our hearts—where the real battle rages. I speak to the Body of Christ, "Have you taken the time to search out all of the things that lie deep within your heart? Do you know the contents and intents of your hearts?" Hebrews 4:12 says, "For the word of God is quick, and powerful, and sharper than any twoedged sword, piercing even to the dividing asunder of soul and spirit, and of the joints and marrow, and is a discerner of the thoughts and intents of the heart."

God is perfect and requires a perfect heart. For this, He has chosen our heart as the place of His presence within us. God would never require from us what He has not already provided. The Word of God reveals the intents and contents of the heart of

God towards man. The Word of God is designed to seed and grow within the heart of man. The Bible voices God's concern, purpose, and intent for mankind. 2 Timothy 3:16-17 states that "All scripture is given by inspiration of God, and is profitable for doctrine, for reproof, for correction, for instruction in righteousness: That the man of God may be perfect, thoroughly furnished unto all good works."

Before salvation, we were filled with evil intents, thoughts, and imaginations, which stemmed from a defiled motive. We were lost until salvation penetrated our heart and, through faith in the Lord, removed the substances of our lost, rebellious, and disobedient hearts. We were provided a new life, a new mind, and a new heart. The Word of God is strictly designed to discern and govern the intents and contents of the heart. If we continue daily in the Word of God, we will eventually possess a Word-filled heart, which is perfect in the sight of God.

If the contents of our hearts are not pleasing to God, the problem and its source must be removed immediately. The intents of our heart determine what the sin is—even if there is no physical "sin act." The intent to sin is seeded within the contents of the heart, which then produces vivid thoughts and imaginations, which results in heart sins and/or outward sins of the flesh. In God's sight, we never have to actually commit the act to be guilty of the crime. Matthew 5:28 gives an example: "But I say unto you, that whosoever looketh on a woman to lust after her hath committed adultery with her already in his heart." This scripture reveals that sin is first an act of the heart. The character, motives, intents, and purposes of the heart are what God judges. Proverbs 23:7 tells us that "as [a man] thinketh in his heart, so is he." That's why it is so very important that what's contained in the Scriptures become firmly rooted in the deep recesses of our hearts. The intent of the heart is the key element that motivates us and wars with us to commit sin. When the heart says "yes," and the soul says "no" or the emotions say "stop," but the mind and flesh say "go forth and commit that sin," we, by our own will, must resist and fight! Scriptural principles must govern our heart's motives in order to provide a shield of protection from the seduction of Code Red and Code Blue sin.

CONTAMINATION BY INFILTRATION

In the beginning, satan, then known as lucifer, was the most beautiful angel in heaven, but one day he thought a wrong thought, which revealed the contents and intents of his heart. His contents became contaminated by his wicked intents, thoughts, desires, and motives. He was then cast out of heaven, and he contaminated a third of the angelic host, taking them with him. "Contaminate" means "to pollute, defile, poison or corrupt," and satan's purpose has not changed. He still seeks to contaminate by infiltration. He uses weapons of lies, fear, lust, sickness, disease, worry, anger, and hate, which are all designed to infiltrate the heart of man, defile its contents, and pollute its intents.

However, God has given us power and authority over satan and his wicked devices. Jesus told us that "Whatsoever we bind on earth, He will bind it in heaven and whatsoever is bound in heaven, we can bind it on earth." I had always thought this scripture was referring to the works of the enemy; however, today I believe Jesus was also talking about satan's heart intents, too. We must bind satan's heart to effectively overcome his evil works. The next time the enemy rises up against you, authoritatively declare "satan, I bind you in your heart." Speaking the Word of God to satan is not enough; he has heard it for thousands of years. Binding his evil works is not enough; he doesn't really care. However, when we rebuke and cast down the intents and desires of his heart, he has to flee. Therefore, secure your heart in the Word of God and build up your heart's defenses with righteousness and holiness. This will effectively cut off the kingdom of darkness.

A CLOSER VIEW OF THE CONTENTS OF OUR HEARTS

The heart is God's creation and design, the engine and life of the human body both naturally and spiritually. It determines purpose, character, destiny and eternal life. The heart is a vessel of extreme intimacy; it contains vast knowledge and unlimited memory base. It is the fountain of wisdom and understanding. The heart makes decisions and holds our purposes, thoughts, and will. Proverbs 27:19 declares "As in water face answereth to face, so the heart of man to man."

I believe this means that when we study our heart our heart studies us; when we look at our heart, it looks back at us. When we speak to our heart, it speaks back to us. God dwells in our heart and is intimately knowledgeable of the true motives and intents of our heart. We need to know what God knows about our heart.

A CLOSER VIEW OF THE INTENTS OF OUR HEARTS

The intents of the heart reflect our desires, motives, and contents and influence the heart towards righteousness or unrighteousness, godliness or ungodliness. Intents and contents are inseparable. A thorough investigation of the contents of the heart will lead to an exploration of the intents as well. Intents are intangible, intense, and powerful. They may be seen within one's character, attitude, and temperament. In the book of Daniel, Daniel was defined as having an excellent spirit because his intent was to please God. Because of this, Daniel was used mightily. Daniel's good intents and contents protected his heart from the Code Blue lion's den he found himself in and was a defense against the enemy's attack on his integrity and service to God. Daniel's intents created a desire to not defile himself with food from the king's table. The contents of Daniel's heart were revealed by his intents to remain faithful and obedient to the will of God. Godly intents of the heart propel us into God's presence and ensures His continued protection as we walk through the valley of the shadow of death, famine, and destruction. Godly intents ensure our eternal position and soundness of character.

YOU MUST BE AUTHENTIC

I found out at a young age that people often appear to be different than they really are. What is seen on the outside may be totally different than what is contained within. Christ described this kind of people in Matthew 13:25-30 as tares. They look like, act like, and talk like, but they are not. More imitators are described in various parts of the Bible.

- False apostles–2 Corinthians 11:13

- Fake teachers–2 Peter 2:1

- Imitation prophets–Matthew 7:15 and 24:11

- Deceptive brethren–Galatians 2:4 and 2 Corinthians 11:26

- False Christ's and witnesses–Matthew 15:19, 24:24, and 26:60

These individuals are not authentic; they give a false report, for they do not have a true heart. They may think their will is religious and that their thoughts and emotions are biblically based, but if they are not properly seeded in true holiness and righteousness, then they are not authentic. Webster's dictionary defines the word *false* to mean "dishonest, untrue, deceptive, and invalid." Moses warned the children of Israel about falseness in Deuteronomy 31:29. Christ also identified false people as wolves in sheep's clothing and as tares to be burned (Matthew 7:15, 13:25-40). These kinds of people are not authentic. They seem to be righteous outwardly, but they are not real inwardly. Inwardly, they are contaminated and defiled. They utter words of falsehood from the heart. They fulfill the words of Isaiah 59:13: "In transgressing and lying against the Lord, and departing away from our God speaking, oppression and revolt, conceiving and uttering from the heart words of falsehood."

The word *authentic* means "true, real, genuine, and reliable." Leaders without an authentic heart have led millions astray, standing in high positions of authority with false hearts. Where there is no authenticity there is no true authority. Without authenticity there is no divine vision or revelation, and without a true vision from a true authentic heart, the people will perish. Many souls have gone to their eternal destiny of damnation believing that they were securely on their way to heaven's glory with the Lord Jesus Christ. They never checked the contents and intents of their own hears to be formally authenticated and heart-approved by God. A heart is right if it is true. There is nothing like the real thing. *Right* means "to be correct, fit, sound, and true." Real is identical in heart with right, for if the heart is not real then it cannot be right. A right heart is mandatory if we want to win battles in Code Red and be victorious in Code Blue. Psalm 78:37 says, "For their heart was not right with him, neither were they stedfast in his covenant." Acts 8:21 states, "Thou hast neither part nor lot in this matter: for thy heart is not right in the sight of God." (See also 2 Kings 10:5.)

God gives His righteousness to the upright in heart (Psalm 36:10). Romans 10:10 tells us that it's with the heart that we believe unto righteousness. We must be right, do right, live right, and be inwardly authentic and correct if we wish to live eternally with Christ. True and right are interchangeable in most cases. The phrase "A true heart that's right" refers to an authentic, sure, valid, right, pure, and clean heart. This is how we must walk in authenticity before Him. Hebrews 10:22 says, "Let us draw near with a true heart in full assurance of faith, having our hearts sprinkled from an evil conscience, and our bodies washed with pure water."

Those with an authentic heart have the anointing to stop the raging river of a Code Red attack or overturn the power and authority of Code Blue. To be authentic as an uncut diamond, the contents of the heart must contain truth. Otherwise, its contents and intents may still be false.

The heart determines who we really are in truth, and the truth is the light that sets the captives caught in Code Red free. None can have an authentic heart without truth. The truth is the key component of every believer's heart. It anchors their soul and determines the real value of the Word of God in their lives. During intense spiritual warfare, we must enter into God's presence and be authentic, speaking the truth *in* our hearts *from* our heart. Psalm 15:2 says, "He that walketh uprightly, and worketh righteousness, and speaketh the truth in his heart."

We must also serve the Lord in truth with all of our heart (1 Samuel 12:24). The truth in God's Word must be the primary content of the heart after the spirit of the Lord himself. No one will ever be free in Code Red without an authentic heart that is full of truth. It's by keeping our hearts pure and truthful that we can enjoy a free heart void of wrong (2 Chronicles 29:31). Even the most precious diamond, if it is cut improperly, will be almost worthless. Our hearts must be circumcised correctly if we are to be valuable treasures. The term "wrong" means "twisted, improper, incorrect, inaccurate, not just, and not right." To defeat the power of Code Red, God sent His Word, the truth, to the earth through the Lord Jesus Christ to firmly establish it in the heart of man.

An authentic heart, with its holy contents, will manifest good intents for us in the midst of Code Red trials. An authentic heart is more precious than all earthly riches and treasures. We secure an authentic heart by strictly obeying God's Word, acting on the Word of God by faith to bring the heart to its full potential (2 Peter 1:5-8).

In spiritual warfare, an authentic heart secures our inward defenses and keeps us holy and pure in God's sight. To build up our spiritual defenses, we must eat of the fruits of the spirit like we eat candy. The fruits of the spirit are love, joy, peace, long suffering, gentleness, goodness, faith, meekness, and temperance (Galatians 5:22-25). Through the fruits and gifts of the spirit, we crucify the flesh where Code Red works to draw us into the evil and dangerous Red Zone. This means in the spiritual there are situations we enter into that are dangerous to our Christian walk that we need to address with God. The gifts of the spirit are the word of wisdom, knowledge, faith, healing, miracles, prophecy, discernment, and tongues. All of these things protect us from the danger of Code Red and Code Blue.

So many people today run into the church from the fear of death, the grave, and hell. They're living in Code Red and being tossed to and fro by the Red Zone. They want religion but not holiness and true biblical salvation. They make the church a social club and not a saving station. They eventually become fake pretenders and shams who have never entered into the true presence of God. They honor the Lord with their hands and lips, but their hearts are far from God. God spoke this to the prophet Isaiah in Isaiah 29:13 and spoke it again through the Lord Jesus Christ in Mark 7:6-7: "He answered and said unto them, well hath Esaias prophesied of you hypocrites, as it is written, This people honoureth me with their lips, but their heart is far from me. Howbeit in vain do they worship me, teaching for doctrines the commandments of men." With raised hands and talking lips these seek to enter behind the veil and worship where he dwells. However none can enter behind the veil into His presence without the Son of God dwelling within the veil of their hearts.

These are the hearts that from all outward appearances look to be on fire with God's Word, His anointing, and truth. These look like the firebrands plucked out of the fire. Amos 4:11 says, "I have overthrown some of you, as God overthrew Sodom and Gomorrah, and ye were as a firebrand plucked out of the burning; yet have ye not returned unto me, saith the Lord." Christ called these kinds of people hypocrites. The term *hypocrite* means "a pretender, deceiver, trickster, swindler, decoy, a masquerader." Hypocrites are like Judas, standing in the sanctuary and sending forth false praise and worship, pretending to give thanks unto the Lord, and faking prayer. They do not have an authentic heart. They are false liars (Revelation 21:8). Christ rejects these people because of their iniquity (Matthew 7:23). Their names are not found in the Lamb's Book of Life (Revelations 20:15). In Luke 11:44, Christ called the Scribes and Pharisees, false religious leaders, hypocrites. In Matthew 6:1-8, He firmly warned His disciples not to pray as the hypocrites do, perform acts to be seen of man, or use vain, repetitious words to pretend to be holy. When God can trust our motives and intents, He gives us peace in the midst of our troubles. There is inner peace when we live by the truth of God's Word.

The soul and mind feast abundantly upon the thoughts and imaginations flowing out of the heart. The heart continues to communicate with God, and God views its intents. As we increase in contents and intents, our conscience also becomes more active, the conscience connects with our emotions, and we are at rest in godliness and contentment in Christ (1 Timothy 6:6). We take up our residence in His presence, we tithe, we continue in His word, and we pray without ceasing, giving thanks to God just because He allows us to see another day. We are authentic. Amen.

4

THOUGHTS AND IMAGINATIONS OF THE HEART

2 Corinthians 10:4-5: *"For the weapons of our warfare are not carnal but mighty through God to the pulling down of strong holds; Casting down imaginations, and every high thing that exalteth itself against the knowledge of God, and bringing into captivity every thought to the obedience of Christ."*

Thoughts are the product of mental activity. A thought is an idea, speculation, perception, notion, contemplation, reflection, rationalization, or recollection (Webster's Dictionary). To think is to consider. Thoughts may be deep or fleeting, and they are the power behind the emotions and the will. Some thoughts are created by the infiltration of spoken words, things we see, feelings, emotions, or the soul. Whether they are good or bad, sinful or holy, our thoughts precede us to our eternal destiny.

Imaginations are thought patterns with good or evil intentions, the faculty of thinking and then knowing. They are the contemplation of actions resulting from the verdict of conscience or the foundation from which desire originates. Imaginations and thoughts may be interchangeable. Imagination brings a verdict with a thought that sets forth the pattern. The phrase "thought patterns" means the design, shape, or model of the mind and heart. In other words, imaginations are thought patterns bought into clear view and are the foundation from which good and evil desires proceed.

I have come to the conclusion that, depending on the condition of our minds, we have the potential to think over 3,000 thoughts and imaginations per day, which equals to approximately

63

one million ninety-five thousand per year. Imaginations are like video's or T.V. pictures manifested within the mind and heart.

Imaginations affect man's emotions, attack the will, rule over desires, and encompass thoughts that bring forth a decision to do, go, stop, utter words, or be still. God hates a heart that devises wicked imaginations as we see in Proverbs 6:16-17: "These six things doth the Lord hate: yea, seven are an abomination unto Him: A proud look, a lying tongue, and hands that shed innocent blood, An heart that devises *wicked imaginations,* feet that be swift in running to mischief" (emphasis added).

No one knows your thought pattern except you, your heart, and God. Thoughts may remain in secret or be expressed openly by body language or through words of the mouth. Thoughts may increase our desires and hinder God's anointing in our lives. Unhealthy thoughts will eat away at our faith.

Thoughts often expand and grow. Expanded evil thoughts consume mental and spiritual space, shutting out blessings, holy thoughts, and spiritual growth. Through the Word of God, these unhealthy thoughts must be cast out for our own safety against Code Red and Code Blue sins. Hebrews 4:12 says, "For the word of God is quick and powerful, and sharper than any twoedged sword, piercing even to the division of soul and spirit, and of joints and marrow, and is a discerner of the *thoughts* and *intents* of the heart" (emphasis added).

The contents of the heart also effect your thoughts. This is the reason we must be filled with the things of God. (Study Hebrews 3:7-19 and Matthew 15:7-20 for more about this.) It is impossible for a living human being not to think a thought. The Bible is a book of thoughts and imaginations written on paper from the heart of God. We ought to fill our minds with the Word of God so that His thoughts become our thoughts.

THINK ABOUT THIS

While we tend to focus on Adam and Eve's act of disobedience, we must also consider why they began to think a new way, which resulted in their doing a new thing. Satan, the first evil and wicked thinker, beguiled Eve with vain, rebellious words, painting a picture with his deceitful words that were designed to poison her mind and spirit. In a matter of moments, Eve processed the thought that changed her thought pattern and expanded her imagination. She was no longer content with being Adam's helpmeet; she wanted to be wiser and live forever. Eve then went to Adam, introduced this new way of thinking, and enticed him the same way she was enticed. With his new thought patterns in control, Adam made the wrong decision and ate of the forbidden fruit. Because man did not have a mediator to intercept sin on his behalf, Code Red sin and Code Blue death were inherently planted in the spiritual genetic code of mankind.

After being banished by God from the Garden of Eden, Adam and Eve bore two sons, Cain and Abel. Cain tended to think evil and wrong thoughts while Abel had good thoughts. God was pleased with Abel and displeased with Cain. Cain killed Abel. What had Cain been thinking prior to this Code Blue deed? God asked Cain where his brother was. Cain thought about it and lied to God, saying, "I do not know!"

Adam and Eve had other children, and mankind began to multiply on the earth. Every man had his own heart, mind, thoughts, and imaginations. Evil thoughts increased; rebellious thoughts soared. Wicked imaginations and evil desires consumed the inward parts of the human race. Every man's heart became defiled, diseased, and clogged beyond repair. God's judgment fell on the whole earth. Man's evil spoken words represented rivers of sinful thoughts. This shows that thought patterns that produce wicked imaginations are serious matters of the heart.

WICKEDNESS OF THE HEART

Genesis 6:5-6: "And God saw that the wickedness of man was great in the earth, and that every imagination of the thoughts of his heart was only evil continually. And it repented the Lord that he had made man on the earth, and it grieved him at his heart."

Continual, hidden evil thoughts and imaginations are Code Red Sin. However, sin is not the greatest issue here; rather, it is the secret evil thoughts and imaginations from within man's heart! This suggests that, before sin can be eradicated, man must receive a new heart and new thought-inducing information from God. No man habitually sins without first thinking about it.

Isaiah 55:7-9 says, "Let the wicked forsake his way, and the unrighteous man his thoughts: and let him return unto the Lord, and he will have mercy on him; and to our God, for he will abundantly pardon. For my thoughts are not yours thoughts, nor are your ways my ways, saith the Lord. For as the heavens are higher than the earth, so are my ways higher than your ways, and my thoughts than your thoughts."

Man habitually seeks after those things that he is not designed to obtain and resists those things that are best for him. He looks for love in all the wrong places, searching for salvation through religion and association instead of a divine relationship with his Creator. Mark 7:21-23 demonstrates this, saying, "For from within, out of the heart of men, proceed evil thoughts, adulteries, fornications, murders, thefts, covetousness, wickedness, deceit, lasciviousness, an evil eye, blasphemy, pride, foolishness: All these evil things come from within, and defile the man."

Man seeks a perfect religion, but God seeks a perfect heart. Man desires to build cities, large churches, and beautiful homes. God seeks to build His church and kingdom within man's heart. Man wants to look good on the outside, but God wants us to be good on the inside. The thoughts and imaginations of our hearts are so out of order that we seek after million dollar titles with 10 dollar hearts. Because of these differences, God's ways are not our ways, and His thoughts are not our thoughts.

God's plan has always been to dwell within the heart of man, but because of the sinfulness of man's thoughts and his imagination to continually do evil, mankind was separated from God. Man willfully chose Code Blue and, because of this heart decision, threw himself into a Code Red State. Mankind, looking to sin rather than to God, is still trying to reach God with an impure heart. Humans have repeatedly looked for ways come to God outside of the Lord Jesus Christ. This, however, cannot be done. Every religion is in desperate need of the heart truth found in God's Word. We cannot continue to serve God from fleshly, finite concepts without the amenity of a pure and clean heart. In fact the word "of God" is the gospel of the heart (Kardiognostes Acts 1:24, 15:8) for our learning- knowledge and understanding of the heart. Many people try to place a comma where God has placed a period, rationalizing the gospel so intently that they have a hundred answers without one true equation. We ignorantly seek our own ways above God's way. John 14:6 says, "I am the way, the truth and the life; no man cometh unto the father, but by me." Jesus Christ stands at the door of every heart to enter therein to set up the most Holy place, redirect man's thoughts and imaginations, and fix every heart for eternal destiny. This is illustrated in Revelations 3:20, which says, "Behold, I stand at the door, and knock: if any man hear my voice, and open the door, I will come into him, and will sup with him, and he with me."

In attempting to reconcile God's truth with our own thoughts and imaginations, we often try to hold Code Blue Sin in our left hand while seeking and striving after God with our right hand. Likewise, we look for external answers when the kingdom of God is within us according to Luke 17:21. We must stop chasing God through our religion if we intend to find Him alive within our hearts. Matthew 6:33 tells us we are to seek first the kingdom of God within our heart. The manifestation of Jesus Christ as the Son of God, the Lord, Messiah, and Savior was God's ultimate divine plan, purpose, and will of His heart for all mankind.

WICKED OR HOLY THOUGHTS

Through Jesus Christ, God's heart can become our heart, and Code Blue will cease to have a stronghold in our lives. Not only does God want our hearts to mirror His, He also desires for our thought patterns to follow His. I believe our God is a God of thought far beyond the understanding of any finite principle. He has personal thoughts of His own, and He also knows what every believer is thinking on the earth at all times. Thoughts have no real power unless they seed and grow in our hearts. Once seeded in the heart of man, like a rising flood, thoughts come creeping into our conscience and senses, overflowing the heart with power, authority, and controlling patterns so awesome that they can overtake us if we are not careful.

In our Christian walk, we face both seen and unseen dangers. Next to the heart itself, the most dangerous enemies to the gospel are not devils and demons, our sin nature, or the flesh. Rather, our thoughts and imaginations, flowing out of the motives and intents of our hearts, represent our second-fiercest foe.

We must remember, then, that we are new creatures created to think on Him, imagine holy things as He does, and act as Christ acted. Wrong thinking caused the fall of both satan and man. Satan thought wrong thoughts, then spoke wrong words, then wanted to do the wrong thing; now he will spend all eternity in the wrong place. Consequently, if we think wrong thoughts, we have the power to do wrong and be wrong. When an unholy thought enters into our hearts and tries to force us into making a wrong decision, we can potentially find ourselves in a serious Code Blue Death grip. No matter how sanctified we are, our hearts will at times be lured by sinful and rebellious thought patterns. But we have a choice. We must capture these wicked thoughts and bring them into the obedience of Christ Jesus. 2 Cor. 10;4-5 gives us perfect instructions as to how we should handle evil thoughts and wicked imaginations. For the weapons of our warfare are not carnal but mighty through god to the pulling down of strongholds, casting down imaginations, and every high thing that exalteth itself against the knowledge of God, and bringing into captitvity every thought to the obedience of Christ. Manifested sin is nothing more than the evidence and fulfillment of evil thoughts and wrong imaginations.

Lest we think that we are fooling God, we must remember that God is omniscient. He is knowledgeable of all our daily thoughts, and He is able to discern our imaginations. He is also aware that the real battle we fight lies within our inner self—the battle between our heart, our thought patterns, our emotions, our imaginations, our will, our mind, and our soul. The outcome of this battle determines whether we walk before God in unrighteousness or righteousness. God wants the Church of the Lord

Jesus Christ to think about what His words say because they are His thoughts to us. If we think on His word, we will not be condemned by wrong words that are the outward result of evil inner thoughts (see Matthew 12:34-37).

LORD, PLEASE FORGIVE ME FOR WRONG THOUGHTS

I remember a time when I was watching my favorite TBN television broadcast on a Sunday night. As I sat in my chair, I beheld several of the ministers laying their hands on people and praying for them. I began to pray, and the Lord spoke to my spirit saying, *"Don, unless these people change their thought patterns, neither prayer nor the laying on of hands will do any good. My son, prayer for the forgiveness of their thoughts and imaginations is what is most needed."* I immediately began to ask God to forgive me for my own thoughts—past and present.

It is of extreme importance that we remain vigilantly aware of our thoughts. Thoughts are prone to change without notice. For example, you might be having a good day when someone delivers extremely bad news to you. Your thought pattern changes, new patterns are formed, new feelings and emotions surge forth, and responses are subsequently formed in the heart. It will take faith and a Word-filled heart to overcome a serious, adverse event. Many times, the only cure from inward confusion is to stay in the presence of God. The Word of God is there not only to enlighten, deliver, and save us, but it is also meant to create new and better thoughts within our hearts. Holy imaginations will produce character, integrity, virtue, dignity, and a better lifestyle.

Keeping a pure and clean heart is the greatest defense against Code Blue Sins. No evil thought or wicked imagination can prosper with a pure and clean heart. The preached Word and the taught Word have power to prick a heart and change our thoughts and imaginations. Meditation in the Word and the daily confession of God's Word will serve as good heart control for the thoughts and imagination. Why does the Lord wish for us to meditate continually on His Word? In deep meditation, new thought patterns and desires are given and received from the believer to God and from God to the believer. Just a few moments of intimate meditations with God can produce enough good thoughts to last for hours, keeping us free from the contamination of this world. It is not enough to give our hearts to Christ; we must also give Him our old thoughts. When we ask God to forgive us of our sins, we should also ask forgiveness for our wrong thoughts and wicked imaginations.

BINDING OUR WRONG THOUGHTS IN THE NAME OF JESUS

We have a powerful weapon against evil thinking—the name of Jesus. It is important that we remember that, if it were not for God's grace and mercy, you and I would be in serious trouble. If He judged us according to our thought patterns, or if our salvation were predicated on our imaginations, we would all most certainly be hell-bound. Thankfully, God's mercy and grace are greater than our sin. It is still important, though, to allow God's thoughts, which are greater than our thoughts, to rule in our lives and replace our old thoughts that produced sin and death. Try visualizing the heart as a thought-and-imagination manufacturing plant in which the soul acts as its storage warehouse. The mind is the generating force; our desires, our will, and our mouth (tongue) are the mind's outlets. The product produced is life or death. While decisions are being made with the will, mind, and soul, right and wrong thoughts and imaginations may be rejected or accepted by the heart. James 1:8 states that a double-minded man is unstable in all his ways. Double-mindedness produces a double heart with double thoughts that allow us to live a double lifestyle. This internal heart-confusion, soul-vexation, and mind-bondage produces a serious inward battle. When the Bible says that the battle is not ours (so stay out of it) but the Lord's, He is simply telling us that it's the inward battle of the Spirit man in which we cannot win without Him. He alone is the heart-fixer and mind-regulator. Only through Him can we have victory over evil thoughts and wicked imaginations of the heart.

SEEKING REST FROM EVIL THOUGHTS AND WICKED IMAGINATIONS

Satan attacks the flesh to get to the heart, to stop our holy thinking, and to destroy or steal God's Word that has been sown and seeded within us (see Luke 8:11-12). Satan's desire is to implant his evil thoughts into our minds, hearts, and souls. However, many times we blame the devil, cast out the devil, and bind the devil *when it is our* flesh, mind, heart, or thought pattern that is in serious need of repair or renewing. When this is the case, we must ask God to capture, arrest, and subdue our wrong thoughts and evil imaginations so that they will not prosper within our heart. Almighty God will bring each one under total subjection, if we through our own will have completely surrendered our lives and hearts to Him. Even though wrong thoughts may enter the mind, a right, pure, and clean heart can dismiss every one of them. The fantastic news is that the Father knows our heart, the Son redeems our heart, and the *Holy Spirit* indwells our heart.

BOUGHT WITH A THOUGHT

One of the six things that God hates (listed in Proverbs 6:18) is the heart that devises wicked imaginations. The Lord wants His thoughts ruling in our minds and hearts. The Holy Spirit is the perfect shield against evil thoughts sent by the enemy. God is a God of thought; He is pleased when His thoughts become our thoughts. He thinks on us. He bought us first with a thought. Jeremiah 29:11-13 says, "For I know the thoughts that I think toward you, saith the Lord, thoughts of peace, and not of evil, to give you an expected end. Then shall ye call upon me, and ye shall go and pray unto me, and I will hearken unto you. And ye shall seek me, and find me, when ye shall search for me with all your heart." Can it be that God wants His people to see as He sees, think as He thinks, hear what He hears, and speak what He speaks? I believe so.

I MUST BE THINKING RIGHT

Repentance that leads to salvation changes your thought patterns. Conviction, like an electrical charge, pricks the wicked mind and evil heart until the sinner exclaims, "Save me Lord; I am willing to obey." An instantaneous change occurs—the sinner becomes a new creature in Christ Jesus. He is given a new heart and a new mind. However, if the mind is not renewed daily, his new heart can revert back to producing evil thoughts. God's

Word is a heart-director and anti-rebellion weapon that is able to cleanse the heart from any residue that a life of Code Red and Code Blue Sin leaves behind.

Faith plays an important part in right thinking. It must not be the outward blessings that increase our faith but the renewing of the mind and the heart. As we walk by faith, we will think in faith, faithfully believing from our hearts. None can be of faith without a faithful heart. Total victory is realized by maintaining pure and clean thoughts. Yes, sanctified thinking is required of true holiness. If any believer is defeated, that defeat is derived from wrong thinking or the increase of wrong thoughts and imaginations in the heart of the believer. Therefore, if you are in defeat, I urge you to evaluate your thought patterns. Paul said in Philippians 4:8: "Finally, brethren, whatsoever things are true, whatsoever things are honest, whatsoever things are just, whatsoever things are pure, whatsoever things are lovely, whatsoever things are of good report; if there be any virtue, and if there be any praise, think on these things." Godly meditation is a great thought defense against wrong thinking. We are commanded to meditate on God's word day and night. Joshua 1:8 says, "This book of the law shall not depart out of thy mouth; but thou shalt meditate therein day and night, that thou mayest observe to do according to all that is written therein: for then thou shalt make thy way prosperous, and then thou shalt have good success." Psalm 1:2 continues, "But his delight is in the law of the Lord; and in his law doth he meditate day and night."

The Word of God, if acted upon, will arrest evil thought patterns. Thought replacement is an area that every believer must seriously commit to seek God. If we think wrong long enough, we begin to believe wrong.

Decide today how you are going to change your thoughts to remove those unwanted patterns of sin. Thought protection is needed for us all. God's holy words defeat evil thoughts and wicked imaginations. His Word restores our hearts.

5

ISSUES AND OPINIONS OF THE HEART

Proverbs 4:23: *"Keep thy heart with all diligence; for out of it are the issues of life."*

Issues are defined as "the act of sending out or putting forth; a going, a departing, a coming, an emerging, a proceeding, a passing, or a flowing out." I believe that issues flow forth as a result of a series of concepts that are printed on the heart, which manifest themselves verbally or physically. Issues from the heart can be positive, such as prayer, worship, and praise, or negative, such as cursing, swearing, and lying.

Opinions are defined as "judgments based on grounds insufficient to produce complete certainty; a personal view, attitude or appraisal; a formal expression or statement; the estimation of a person or a thing according to character or merit." An opinion is what one *thinks* about an issue, but the truth is what a person *knows* about an issue. An opinion can also be described as a guess regarding a view or concern as opposed to faith, which believes that concern has already been taken care of according to God's Word.

THE POWER OF ISSUES AND OPINIONS

There are two basic types of issues: good or bad and right or wrong. In error, we try to "make sense" of a bad issue and work out a wrong issue without God. What "makes sense" to man is almost always nonsense in God's sight. When we try to "make sense," of something on our own, deep thought patterns come forth that are formed by opinions. Issues, then, should only be viewed in context of the Word of God. Every human being on earth is engulfed in his or her own opinions. A writer once stated that "opinions are as ears; everybody has them." Like the heart, opinions may argue with true facts. While we do enjoy freedom, we as Christians need to be more reserved and self-conscious concerning our opinions. They force us to make serious decisions about serious issues, which is why they must be kept subject to God's Word.

Within our spirit man is a volatile element of great power—the opinion. Opinions can encompass our total being and powerfully guide our thoughts, our minds, our wills, our emotions, and our hearts. An opinion rules, directs, and manifests itself through the power of our heart. Silently and oftentimes secretly, opinions spring forth without warning. They are powerful, personal, or impersonal elements that come from the heart and mold our character. Opinions have the power to alter our state of mind, change our nature, direct our decisions, and determine our life's destination. Their origin is without complete knowledge; their formation and structure cannot be fully identified. We do know that a child of just a few months has the capability to communicate his opinion before he can utter his first words.

Opinions have their root, power, and seed in the heart. People voice their opinions, whether they are incorrect or correct. Opinions can oppose the mind, soul, and even God's Word. They may be evil, wicked, unrealistic, unreasonable, unwarranted, or unwanted. They can control our feelings, emotions, and desires, while directing many thoughts of our hearts. They confuse the mind and never meet the complete needs of the soul. Opinions may be outright lies, or the result of deception. Opinions may determine the length of a marriage, the success of a sports figure, your paycheck, and personal hygiene. They may act as the supreme judge and jury in our lives, but yet remain in secret. No one can flee from their own opinions.

Both the unsaved and saved can be bound, seduced, and guided by their opinions, even if those opinions are in contrast to God's Word. Therefore, correct opinions are crucial and require a right estimation, viewpoint, regard, judgment, and evaluation. God expects for us to have high opinions of Him and each other. He fashions our new hearts so that good opinions may issue forth. Right opinions tend to dispel bad issues. Wrong opinions lead our heart to make bad decisions, utter negative faithless words, thus hindering our walk with God.

God's opinion of you and me is the most valuable opinion of all. God showed us plainly his opinion of Code Red Sin and Code Blue Death by and through the life and death of Christ. We keep His opinion of us high when we obey His Word and walk by faith in love toward each other. Believers of all denominations need to change their opinion of each other, for the better, so that unity and peace may increase and love may be magnified in the Body of Christ. If we want our needs, desires, and plans to be met and fully materialized in this life, we must monitor the issues and opinions flowing continually out of our hearts. Issues and opinions determine prayer life, health life, salvation, deliverance and even divine healing. God is greater than the issues and opinions of our heart. The heart is the key, for it is the heart's condition that determines our ability to think holy thoughts, live holy lives, enjoy godly thoughts, make right choices, and avoid bad issues and opinions.

The key difference between issues and opinions is the fact that issues are tangible, while opinions are intangible. Issues come from deep-seated places in the heart. Things that issue forth from an evil heart may include murder, rape, incest, sickness, and disease. These are Code Blue issues. Opinions also lie within the heart, just waiting to explode forth. However, they cannot be seen, felt, and touched. A good antidote for wrong opinions is to be obedient and faithful, having a mind that is made up for Jesus Christ. The Holy Spirit can then work with us, helping to lead us to right decisions and helping us avoid issues that divide and wrong opinions that bind. We must never lean on our own understanding, knowledge, or feelings, but in all our ways acknowledge Jesus Christ (Proverbs 3:6). I personally believe (it's my opinion) that one of the main reasons opinions have such great control and power is that very few people pray for the heart of their fellow believers, their mates, and their children. This is serious.

Salvation gives believers brand new opinions and, in time, new and better issues. God changes the sinner's opinions and heals their bad issues. This is how we can boldly say we're saved. The new life in Christ through salvation has given us a better way with new opinions and new issues of life. Opinions of the heart are in the church every Sunday. They determine the value of the preacher's message, the amount of tithes given, the songs of the choir, and the levels of praise and worship. Heart opinions may be hot or cold and have the power to stop the continual flow of blessings. Some opinions and issues are positive, but some are very negative. Some negative opinions have cost people their lives. For example: many are of the opinion that they don't need the Holy Spirit to be saved or that Jesus Christ is not the Lord or that that there is no God. Negative opinions produce low self-esteem, anti-God thoughts, and low self-worth attitudes in many hearts. Many have taken their own lives due to bad issues and negative opinions. A voiced opinion may devastate one's life if it is seeded from the heart. God has imparted forgiveness and repentance in the earth through Christ so that evil opinions and wicked issues won't rule over mankind. Even the vilest persons on earth have the power to ask for forgiveness. True forgiveness eliminates the effects of bad issues. Bad issues and wrong opinions separate a Christian from right fellowship and their daily communication with God.

IT'S YOUR ISSUE THAT'S MY OPINION

Opinions seeded in the heart can be very powerful, especially when debating an issue. Issues in debate may become so intense that the person debating walks away angry stating firmly, "That's my opinion and I'm not going to change it." A tender heart from God, or a new heart, helps us rid ourselves of opinions that are not approved of God. Approved opinions agree with the Word of God. Disapproved opinions relative to the Word of God are often manifestations of rebellion and disobedience. The more we walk in the truth through love and faith, the more right opinions will flourish. If we work diligently to maintain right opinions from our heart, victory will also prevail. We must understand that loss or defeat don't always come from our enemy. Sometimes they come by and through the bad opinions that we hold on to, despite knowing that they are wrong. Godly opinions are available for every man. God doesn't want any of his people to fall into an opinionated state. We must walk by faith, not by opinions. Wrong opinions that emulate forth from our hearts can cause issues to come to life and seed within those opinions. Evil opinions seeded in the heart are very difficult to remove. Those who know Christ and still commit various Code Red sins such as adultery, abortion, fornication, and rebellion have altered opinions that only the Lord can change.

Issues and opinions, whether holy or unholy, are the result of many thoughts and imaginations that are the result of the contents and intents of the heart. This is nothing new. In Old Testament times, when the wicked thoughts and imaginations of man's heart were continually evil, God's opinion of the sin issue and the condition of man's heart moved Him to destroy all living things, except Noah and his family, through the flood. God had a low opinion of man's issues, which He judged to be beyond repair, so He sent the flood. This world continues to operate in an evil, controversial state of no return, building up more wickedness each day and awaiting God's wrath to fall.

Christians must be separate from the world. God isn't just our heart-fixer and mind-regulator, but He (knowing all about our opinions and issues) becomes our heart sealant and sealer, sealing us against the wiles, tricks, and fiery darts of all our enemies. We must submit ourselves to God and make sure that we agree with Him. The power of agreement nullifies the effects of adverse opinions and hurting issues. God extends forgiveness and intercessory prayer to destroy those issues and bad opinions brought on by envy, debate, strife, controversy, and hate. Wisdom and understanding are helpful in cases in which the heart is overcome by fear, doubt, insecurity, and unbelief. Know this: if one lives on this earth, both evil and good will soon come. It's all about how we receive that good or evil, the strength of our heart in light of blessings or challenges, and what opinions we'll have about them when they arrive.

FORMING RIGHT OR WRONG OPINIONS

As a newborn child grows to the tender age of two or three months, knowledge comes and opinions begin to flow forth from the heart. At the age of approximately nine months, a child can make decisions, and from one to two and a half years all types of issues begin to evolve and manifest themselves in the heart of a child. Rebellion, disobedience, and deception, when manifested, separate children from the will of God and from the will of their parents. Opinions have the power to hold a soul bound from the crib to the grave. By the time one reaches the age of 21, they are well-developed in opinions, issues, and controversies, but yet they do not know their own heart. But if we train up our children in the way they should go, according to the Word of God, they will have a better handle on life when they reach adulthood.

The heart training of a child depends not only upon the Lord, but also upon the opinions of the parents. If the family isn't one in Christ, the wife's opinion may differ on how the child is to be raised from that of her husband's. A controversy develops. Anguish of heart, hurting words, dishonor and no respect begin to seed and rule. If there is repentance, the Holy Spirit will move to change the texture of the issues and restore the good opinions that were lost. Parents need to know—and believers need to be reminded—that God's Word never tells us what to do without also telling us how to do it, or have us to walk in a way that we know not. It's the Word in action in our lives that acts as our opinion guide and issue deliverer.

In every city, country, prison, court, and walk of life there are highly opinionated people living by their own heart issues of life. Even Christians sometimes allow their own opinions to control them, rather than allowing themselves to be controlled by the Holy Spirit. High, wrong opinions dishonor God, and continual sinful thoughts and worldly desires lead our footsteps quickly out of God's will. All heart issues of life, such as holiness, righteousness, and truth, necessitate that you and I remain spiritually in control. Our life is hid in Christ, and we will never eternally die. But, just as there are issues of life, there are also issues of death, such as Code Red Sin, all unrighteousness, rebellion, and disobedience. As sinners, we were Code Blue Dead through the payment of Christ's blood at Calvary, we can now have life. Psalm 68:20 illustrates this, saying, "He that is our God is the God of salvation; and unto God the Lord belong the issues from death."

SERIOUS ISSUES

Just as all opinions are not evil and bad, neither are all issues. It's how one views or perceives an issue that determines the quality of the opinions formed by that particular issue. In fact, it's the opinion about an issue and the heart's concern for that issue that will determine the magnitude of the issue.

Heart issues of life are the greatest issues on earth. In the Scriptures, issues are sometimes called a matter or a controversy. Prophets, priests, kings, and laymen worked continuously to settle matters (issues) that were crucial to their existence. While an opinion may remain in secret for years, it is much harder for issues to remain quiet. They are often explosive, causing division, decay, and, in some cases, Code Blue Death. Certain issues may hinder spiritual growth, wound the spirit man, or cause the most faithful church member to leave in disgust, lay down his or her Bible, cease to pray, and even return to a life of Code Red Sin.

An issue is always the prime root of divorce, separation, or rejection and may come before or after an established opinion. Issues can kill, steal, consume, and destroy a whole family, church group, community, or even a nation. Issues are matters, situations, and concepts. What matters to us become what concerns us most. Our concerns then become issues that set up situations that bring forth debate, division, and confusion both inwardly and outwardly. To be divided about any issue, regardless of its nature, is not healthy. For example, if our mind, soul, and body needs rest, but the heart's will and desires say no, immediately there's an issue of whether to rest or not. A small inward war develops, and there's no rest for the victim that night until the issue has been resolved. Unresolved issues have been the basic cause for all sorts of problems, ranging from family division to world wars. Unresolved issues of the heart cause our emotions to attack our will and our desires to assail our minds, while our souls speak to our hearts saying, "I've had enough" or "I quit." The most serious problem has no real power until it develops opinions within the heart and is made into a real issue in our lives.

The key to winning the wars pertaining to thoughts, opinions, and issues in life is found in scripture. Keep good things in your heart, regardless of adverse circumstances. When the Holy Spirit inhabits a person, He imparts spiritual fruit to counteract negative issues of life. Godly matters such as love, joy, salvation, and wisdom should never be seen as undesirable issues by the saved believer. What must we do to obtain these issues? Philippians 4:8-9 advises all to do this: "Finally, brethren, whatsoever things are true, whatsoever things are honest, whatsoever things are just, whatsoever things are pure, whatsoever things are lovely, whatsoever things are of good report; if there be any virtue, and if there be any praise, think on these things. Those things, which ye have both learned, and received, and heard, and seen in me, do: and the God of peace shall be with you."

Matters (issues) that face a person on any given day may be small, great, hard, good, easy, right, or wrong, and they may release many opinions. God's heart contains nothing but good matters (issues) of concern for all of his children. Every opinion does not necessarily contain issues within it, but issues may consist of many opinions. However, if something catastrophic occurs, opinions will spring forth along with many issues. In the death of a wife, family member, or church member, many opinions and issues may arise. Terrorists who attacked the World Trade Center on September 11th were not only lost sinners, but they also held a very low opinion of America. Their issues destroyed their own lives, along with many others. The entire unsaved world has issues with Christians and with God, and it can't wait to voice its wrong opinions. Most of this world's population has an issue with God, directly or indirectly. Satan has an issue with God; therefore, he automatically has one with God's people, and we should have many with him, including a very low opinion. Stem cells, same-sex marriages-abortions-cloneing though they are all great issues they **must** be held in very low opinions. We must not pass laws that legalizes sin. These issues are against Gods purpose-plans and word. Ultimately they will produce more sin and death. That's my opinion.

Issues also affect the state of our mind and heart, setting up their overall state and condition. A clean mind and a pure heart are the result of the operations of God, just as an evil mind and a wicked heart are the result of allowing anti-God principles to be in control. No man can overcome bad issues and opinions by employing an evil heart and a wicked mind. Bad issues don't need to be voiced because the more an issue is voiced, the more it is magnified. If a person isn't saved or living a holy life, he has a direct, adverse issue with God. A sinning heart has a continual flow of the issues of death rather than the issues of life. Proverbs 4:23 says, "Keep thy heart with all diligence; for out of it are the *issues of life*" (emphasis added). Believers must consider their opinions daily, continually analyzing all issues very thoroughly. For their heart's sake, they must try to always think, act, and make correct decisions according to the Word of God.

THE ISSUES OF LIFE

The issues of life are always real matters of the heart. Issues flowing from a true believer's heart are awesome, positive, and great. As they come forth from the heart, they set forth thought patterns, desires, decisions, controversies, and opinions that decide the total outcome about issues. However, they all require high opinions in order to function and manifest properly. Issues and opinions address broken promises, procedures and disputes in the workplace, heated arguments, opposition to laws passed, disagreements in marriages, relationships that release much

81

internal stress, worry, fear, and confusions producing diseases, and, for some, Code Blue Death. They can divide and separate the church. Let Jesus Christ be your guide when it comes to issues, and let Him always be the highest opinion that you have in this life.

Since the day of my salvation, I've found myself in disagreements over matters, issues, and controversies that are far too great for me. As I continue daily in God's Word and grow in Christ, some have been resolved, but many seem to grow with me. My own opinions and issues would consume my life if I did not go to the throne of grace with fasting and prayer, asking the Lord to loose and deliver me from my own opinions and the issues of my heart. He responds that I must keep my mind stayed on Him, place my heart in His hands, and walk by faith in obedience to His Word. I have found him to be a God who is well able to resolve my issues and change my heart's opinions.

As an example of the kind of issue with which Christians sometimes grapple, let's look at the issue of titles that church leaders take unto themselves. Titles such as pastor, bishop, apostle, deacon and usher may present great controversial problems if they are not ordained of God and seasoned in the heart. We, as God's leaders, must increase in love, faith, and wisdom so that foolish and harmful issues such as this will cease to rule in the house of God. For example, we know that many believe that a woman cannot call herself bishop or pastor; however if she is married to a bishop, pastor, or other leader, she must have the same knowledge as her husband in order to properly advise, support, and be the spiritual helpmate required. The leader and his wife are one in God's eyes, both with the same spiritual ability and power. Both are one in heart. Ultimately, it's what God calls us and not what man ordains that's the most serious. What man thinks is not what God thinks. His thoughts and opinions are not influenced by the doctrines of man. Man ordains into a title or office, but God ordains in heart and spirit. That's my opinion. Therefore, if you should ever meet a woman pastor or bishop, do not allow her title to become an issue between you.

Interpretation of scripture, pulpit exercises, and church service procedures are further examples of real issues and deep controversies faced by churches today. They separate and divide most clergy. While I enjoy a quiet service and a speaker who speaks softly and eloquently, I also love to rejoice, shout, and give high praises to God with those who leap high or run through the aisles as a wild person out of control. Radical praisers lose their common sense to gain God sense. They fall on the floor, slain in the spirit, speaking in an unknown tongue. Oh, issue-laden believer, don't you know that God is still in control? In the end, it's His will that must be done. And ultimately, it is not the issues that matter; it is God that matters.

If the Church be destroyed in the earth, it will be because of many bad issues, evil thoughts, and wrong opinions! Dwelling on hot issues and constantly voicing contrary opinions causes anger to arise. This brings division and hurt. The Apostolic Church of the Lord Jesus Christ as a whole does not believe in women preachers, yet I've heard women preach three-minute sermonettes called "testimonies." They don't believe that women should be pastors, yet women minister in song at every service. Many things that man rejects, God accepts. The c.o.g.i.c. (Church of God In Christ) faith does not believe in women preachers (as of 1997), yet since their beginning female missionaries went out and preached and were accepted. The body parts of the female genda was never created to determine their walk and call of God. All true sermons and titles must be God-given, approved, and ordained. The main concern should be this: is there any manifestation of the spirit of God for salvation, deliverance, and healing? If so, the woman preacher who preaches so that souls come forth for salvation must not be thought of as an issue, but as a joy. We should be more concerned about God's opinion of His female servants than we are with our own opinions.

Issues also often arise due to differences among denominations. Even though I am a pastor in the church of the Lord Jesus Christ of the Apostolic Faith, I love to preach in all churches that call on the name of Jesus Christ. I refuse to be laden with divisions and issues that kill, steal, and destroy, causing many who are called to fall from God's presence. These issues can only be solved by God. I personally know many anointed, called, and chosen people of God who are afraid to "go forth" and answer their call due to doctrinal issues set up by church leadership. Rather than be defeated by issues, we should follow the advice of Acts 5:29, which says," We ought to obey God rather than men."

PROTECT (KEEP) THY HEART

Because issues and opinions ultimately come from the heart, it's very important that we learn to monitor and control our hearts' input and output channels. These channels are the eyes, ears, and mouth. Satan monitors the input and output channels of every sinner's heart, and God does the same with the hearts of His saints. The enemy, by using issues and opinions, seeks to infiltrate the hearts of believers with his poisonous principles, knowing that the heart will send out whatever it holds or receives within. What we allow to be sown in our hearts will eventually manifest in our lifestyle. This is why Proverbs instructs us to keep, or guard, our hearts with all diligence (Proverbs 4:23).

The term *heart infiltration* can be used to describe the practice of someone or something penetrating and filling the heart with either evil or good. If envy infiltrates the heart, it is reproduced and sent forth as jealousy, covetousness, resentfulness, greed, craving, spite, grudge bearing, prejudice, or malice. It stifles the mind, causing morbid accumulations of thoughts, issues, and opinions that are detrimental to its victim. Whereas satan seeks to infiltrate and pervade without right or notice, Christ isn't a heart stealer but a heart keeper and doctor. Christ doesn't enter our hearts by infiltration but by invitation. With our heart's doors opened by repentance, He comes in with power and the right issues of life, releasing from within himself right opinions and sowing divine issues into our hearts. On the other hand, satan wants to fill our hearts with evil purposes and controversies that cause heated issues and wicked opinions to spew forth from us. He fills many hearts by encompassing them with

84

wrong opinions and by making good issues seem bad. By infiltrating the heart, satan becomes a heart thief, a mind robber and a soul burglar.

The most horrible thing is to see satan succeed in infiltrating the hearts of Christians, convincing them that wrong opinions about things such as legalized abortion, gay rights, human rights, civil rights, and women's rights are in fact right. Only God's word is right, regardless of opposing opinions. It's time that we used personal "mouth control" and learn how to disagree agreeably. An example from Acts 5:1-5 shows us what can happen when we allow satan to invade our hearts. "But a certain man named Ananias, with Sapphira his wife, sold a possession, and kept back part of the price, his wife also being privy to it, and brought a certain part, and laid it at the apostles' feet. But Peter said, Ananias, why hath s*atan filled thine* heart to lie to the Holy Ghost, and to keep back part of the price of the land? While it remained, was it not thine own? and after it was sold was it not in thine own power? why hast thou conceived this thing in thine heart? thou hast not lied unto men, but unto God. And Ananias hearing these words fell down, and gave up the ghost: and great fear came on all them that heard these things" (emphasis added).

The book of Job provides another example of issues and opinions that are out of control and out of God's will. In Job 32 through 37, we read not only of Job's popular three friends but of an unpopular fourth man named Elihu, who kept silent throughout Job and his three friend's recitation of their evil issues and opinions of Job's circumstances. Job was judged to be righteous by his three friends Eliphaz, Bildad, and Zophat, who had the wrong opinion of God. However, it was Elihu, the youngest of them all, who had the right attitude about God and the correct opinion, which pleased God. Therefore, Elihu acted as God's representative. At the end, God chastened Job and his three opinionated friends but not Elihu, which should teach us to be careful about the opinions and issues we voice. Job's three friends had high opinions of themselves, but a low opinion of Job, which illustrates that the only time you need to look down upon a man is when you're lifting him up. The name Elihu means, "He is my God." Job 32:6,10, 11, and 17 say, "And Elihu the son of Barachel the Buzite answered and 'said I am young, and ye are very old; therefore I was afraid, and durst not shew you mine opinion.' Therefore I said, 'Hearken to me; I also will shew mine opinion. Behold, I waited for your words; I gave ear to your reasons, whilst ye searched out what to say. I said, I also will answer my part, I also will shew mine opinion'" (see Job 33:3, 37:1).

In the text that follows the cited passage in Job, Elihu gives the godly perspective and glorifies God. Job's other three friends, like most of us, were too hasty to utter their private views, analyses, and opinions of God in regard to Job's dilemma. On the other hand, Elihu spoke by the leading of the Holy Sprit, revealing truth and showing us the right way to approach all adverse situations that may be deeply embedded in wrong issues and wicked opinions (see Job 42:1-3). I believe that the bottom line is this: Whatever you do or are doing and whatever you say or have said, make sure that God is pleased, and make sure your love for God and man is strong enough to keep God's wrath from falling upon your life. Fear God and keep His commandments.

NOTICE TO BELIEVERS: GUIDELINES REGARDING ISSUES AND OPINIONS

A. Opinions should be voiced only through the eyes of love, and issues—whatever they may be—should be discussed in light of biblical principles. Always stop, look, and listen.

B. Increased faith and love always deliver us from bad opinions as we're commanded to walk by faith and not by sight (2 Corinthians 5:7). Whatever isn't of faith is sin (Romans 14:23). Faith works by love (Galatians 5:6), and love works the heart. Therefore, always keep a favorable respect for views of others.

C. Form all your opinions by the manifestation of faith through the eyes of love. Approach your daily issues by asking God for more love, wisdom, and understanding. Stand on God's Word on every issue.

D. Voice God's opinion in all issues and matters of importance, and lean not on your own understanding, feelings, or emotions. When caught up in issues that are heated, heavy, or hateful, act according to God's Word, walk uprightly, and keep a good opinion regardless of the consequences or circumstances.

E. Remember how Elihu voiced God's opinion in contrast to Job and his friends, who voiced their own. Make God's choice your choice. The closer we walk with Christ, the better our opinions will be and the fewer issues we'll face. He promised us that if our ways pleased Him that He would make our enemies at peace with us (Proverbs 16:7). The better the opinion, the greater the heart.

F. Search for truth, which is the actual state of the matter, conformity with fact or reality, and a verified or indisputable fact or principal. Choose honesty, integrity, correctness, fidelity, authenticity, and accuracy.

As we daily conform to God's Word and His will, the Lord will fervently work on us to effect change. He will eliminate in order to elevate. Total heart transformation will render all of us perfect in the sight of God. Why are many believers not yet perfect? The issues of sin and the sin condition of the heart prevent maturation and perfection. Active, committed sins are always issues of the heart and life. Even a person who is pure in heart will immediately have an issue of the heart if he or she begins to plan, meditate on, or commit a Code Red sin. Sin issues of the heart mean an outward flowing of an ungodly pattern.

Daily issues of the hidden man of the heart are far too numerous for our finite minds to number and remember. Only God knows. I believe that before true deliverance can take root, there first must be a setting free from issues and opinions of the heart. But with Christ alive in our hearts, no matter the issue, controversy, or opinion, there is hope. We have faith, for we know that He is able to perform all that He has promised in His Word.

Thanks be to God for His love and grace with mercy to help when the issues of the heart become a heavy weight. When it comes to your heart, don't settle for second best. It's walking in the love of God that keeps our hearts settled, safe, and secure in God (see 1 John 3:18-22). Love is God's very best stronghold against serious issues and opinions of the heart.

6

THE NEGATIVE AND THE POSITIVE HEART

Many believers are unaware of the hidden struggle between the positive and the negative. This has been evident since the beginning of man and most likely will only intensify until the Lord's return. The positive builds faith, but the negative works to destroy faith. The problem lies deep within the heart, which has much experience with both the negative and the positive. The heart is like a potter's vase. It can be fashioned (molded) into that which displeases God or fashioned to please God.

Our words, whether they are positive or negative, often reflect the true state of the heart. Positive or negative words can also impact the state of the heart. Many have fallen from a high, positive position into a low state of doubt, unbelief, and confusion due to the power of negative words. God's Word is always positive, but the words we speak—if they are out of sync with God's Word, will, and purpose for our lives—will place our destiny in jeopardy.

God recognizes the power of the tongue (see James 3) and wants His people to restructure their vocabulary to encompass the positive utterances that build and edify our faith while abolishing the negative words that work to steal, kill, and destroy our faith. Being positive not only helps to develop our attitude and our Christian character, it also releases the power of goodness into our daily lives. We are creatures of habit, but our spiritual heart is an element of purpose—it holds our plans and determines our destiny.

Negative words have caused many people to remain lost. How is this? Out of the heart the mouth speaks (see Matthew 12:34), and by our words (see verse 37) we are either justified or condemned.

Words mold and fashion the heart as well as the faith by which we daily trust in God. Pure faith requires that we speak positive words of faith and completely avoid the negative. All things that are negative are enemies of faith.

Webster's Dictionary defines the word *positive* to mean "precise, confident, affirmative; having the mind and heart set and settled." We attribute the same meaning to the following: "yea," "amen," "I will," "I can," "I am," "yes," and "I do." The term *negative* is defined as "expressing denial or refusal that always says no; lacking in positive character, evidence, and affirmation; or having a diminishing, depriving, or denying effect." The following expressions support this meaning: "not so," "I cannot," "I am not," and "I will not." Negative words reject or refuse.

Negativity can take many forms, but it always produces negative results. All too often, without considering the price, we say "No, I can not teach," "I will not study my Bible or pray today," or "No, I will not go to church tonight." All the while, these negative words have begun to seed, grow, and manifest power within the heart.

Our daily vocabulary is often an indication of what is seeded and rooted in the heart. Jesus warned us about our word vocabulary in Matthew 12:34-37, which says, "O generation of vipers, how can ye, being evil, speak good things? for out of the abundance of the heart the mouth speaketh. A good man out of the good treasure of the heart bringeth forth good things: and an evil man out of the evil treasure bringeth forth evil things. But I say unto you, That every idle word that men shall speak, they shall give account thereof in the day of judgment. For by thy words thou shalt be justified, and by thy words thou shalt be condemned."

Jesus' words cut to the core of the issue. I believe that it's time for every believer to address his or her word choices in God's presence to examine the true state of his or her heart.

As lost sinners, it was natural for us to speak using a negative vocabulary, which reflected and/or produced a lifestyle that was sinful. However, now that we're born again, we should use a positive vocabulary consisting of "Yes Lord," "I will, God," and "Amen." God is never negative. He demands that we be completely positive. Being positive is a great attribute, and it reflects God's nature rather than the sinful nature.

Because the heart always retains our words, continually holding knowledge of what we do or say, we must monitor everything to which we allow our hearts to be subject. Words condition the heart, and out of the heart our mouth speaks. God never takes away the freedom we have in choosing whether or not to implement His will; rather, He allows us to choose between negative words, which may become as iron bars around our necks, stumbling blocks in our pathway, and chains on our tender feet and faithful, positive words, which build a strong foundation within us. This solid infrastructure allows us to be fashioned in the way of a true Christian disciple having a righteous disposition.

If we speak negative words when the positive is needed, we find ourselves outside of the will of God. Through many negative utterances, a negative heart is formed. When we are bound by a negative heart, there can be no spiritual growth. Blessings become rare, and the true power of a saved lifestyle is seldom seen or enjoyed. It is time for the church to teach a positive gospel and show a positive program so that believers may rid themselves of their powerful negative vocabularies. Our words represent a very serious matter of the heart because if we speak negatively in response to God's will or purpose, our words may eventually lead to Code Blue Death.

BE POSITIVE FOR SURE

The only time a believer should utter negative words is when he or she is using them to reject sin or temptation. I do not

91

want to give the impression that only words with an inherently positive meaning should come forth from our mouths. Rather, sometimes it is necessary for words that are negative—such as "no"—be used to bring about a positive result. Sometimes, we may use words that appear to be negative on the surface, but are positive in light of what is being presented, rejected, or denied, such as "No, I will not tell a lie." When our heart responds to God's calling, let our words resound with a positive "yes," "all right, Lord," "amen," "I can," "I will," and "I am." However, when we are tempted to sin, we must use negative words such as "no," and "I will not" to resist temptation.

A negative heart that repeatedly says "No," "I cannot," or "I will not" to God's divine will or purpose will soon find itself in a state of confusion, causing backsliding, depression, trouble, or some other type of Code Red Sin to seriously affect one's Christian demeanor (conduct or behavior). Therefore, it is imperative for all who live in Christ to respond to Him with positive words that reflect a positive heart. Be not deceived: the choice between the positive and the negative is always ours to choose. Two of the smallest words, yes and no, are also two of the strongest, most powerful words in the English language. They are so powerful that even God bases our relationship with Him on these two simple words. These words both hold significant power in the heart. Therefore, when it comes to God, we must choose the positive "yes" every time.

THE REMEDY FOR NEGATIVITY

A negative attitude that is developed and governed by a negative heart will hinder positive faith. Positive faith encompasses our positive character, which assures us of being in God's favor and perfect will. Bad character produces a bad attitude, which puts limits on God. It hinders us from knowing God, loving Him, and doing His perfect will. A bad, negative character or attitude renders its victim loveless, trustless, blessingless, and useless. A negative attitude produces confusion, division, anger, and rage, and it brings grief to the Holy Spirit. What is the antidote for bad character and a negative attitude? We must be broken for the Master's use. We must allow God, who is the Great Physician, to work with His loving hands to perform brokenness within us as needed. Complete brokenness, which means we are subdued, trained, and tamed by God, will also destroy sin, lust, rebellious-ness, and condemnation. Brokenness destroys the power of pride and self-will and softens the hardness of the heart. Once broken-ness is complete, God can then build our personality, character, constitution, attitude, and temperament, which will in turn affect the words we speak. If a person does not respond positively to God's voice, a bad temperament and disposition, resulting from a negative heart, can cause adverse spiritual and physical health conditions. Rebelliousness, disobedience, and stubbornness may then be locked in the realm of our temperament.

CHOOSING A POSITIVE HEART

Again, we have a choice. We can allow the Lord Jesus Christ, through His Word, love, and Spirit, to temper us, or we can allow satan to control our temperament. If we give Jesus control so that temperance, brokenness, and character can be firmly set, we become free from all strongholds of the enemy that would keep us in a negative minus rather than a positive plus. I want to mention here that a stronghold is not necessarily negative in and of itself; rather, it is our attitude toward that stronghold that deems it neg-ative or positive. Through the power of repentance, strongholds can be turned into a plus. Some negative strongholds are the love of money, fear, lust, sickness, disease, rebelliousness, and ungodly anger. Positive strongholds (fortresses) such as love, peace, faith, wisdom, and God's Word are sound defenses against both Code Blue and Code Red Sins. God himself, however, is our greatest fortress, and in Him alone can we trust. Psalm 18:2 says, "The Lord is my rock, and my fortress, and my deliverer; my God, my strength, in whom I will trust; my buckler, and the horn of my sal-vation, and my high tower." (See Psalm 91:2 for more on this.)

Since God is our fortress when we become born again, we must continually check ourselves to be sure that our hearts are

93

safe within His walls of protection. Before we were saved, our negative hearts were full of sin, which produced cursing, swearing, other negative utterances, and an ungodly lifestyle in general. Now that we have been delivered from this negative existence, do we now show forth a saved character, a holy constitution, a godly attitude, a righteous disposition, and a positive demeanor? If not, what must we do? We must control our mouths, seek to use positive words, and constantly monitor the state of our heart. When we do this, we will begin to exemplify the kind of positive, godly lifestyle that is pleasing to God.

Many people claim to be new creatures in Christ while still clinging to negative attitudes within their hearts. However, a negative heart is not a new heart in Christ. It is still out of order, and if it remains so, it causes the character and spiritual constitution to remain out of order as well. This in turn causes spiritual sickness. Can a believer be born again and have spiritual sickness? I believe so. It is caused by negative doubt and unbelief that is allowed to take seed as a tare within us. Christ told us to take His yoke upon us and learn of Him (Matthew 11:29-30). Why? He is the only way to the Father for truth, life, and spiritual health. Any other way will produce negativity, sickness, or Code Blue Death of some kind. Seeking heart deliverance will be mandatory. Until we learn of Him, grow in Him, and allow ourselves to be completely transformed into His perfect image, we are at risk. We can remain negative and spiritually sick in our heart, mind, thoughts, and emotions, having a bad attitude and poor Christian character that hold on to an ungodly disposition. Though we are saved, the mind, heart, and soul can become sick. This sickness can take many forms and may produce adulterous pastors, gay ministers of music, lying deacons, and fornicating saints. While living sinful lifestyles, they give praise and worship to God singing "Oh, how I love Jesus." These kinds of sicknesses are very serious matters of the heart. Isaiah 1:5 says, "Why should ye be stricken any more? Ye will revolt more and more: the whole head is sick, and the whole heart faint. (Also see Jeremiah 5:23-25.)

DON'T BE A NAY-SAYER

The negative heart disagrees with almost everything somebody else is saying while rarely having anything good or positive to say. I call people with this kind of heart nay-sayers. In the Old Testament, Moses sent Joshua and Caleb to spy out the Promised Land of milk and honey. There were some nay-sayers who went with them and returned with an evil, negative report. However, Joshua and Caleb brought back a good, positive report. The nay-sayers said "We can not go," "We will not," "We should not," and "No, not us." They never went, and God rejected them. Years prior to this incident, God delivered Israel out of Egypt by parting the Red Sea. Israel went across on dry ground, but there were still nay-sayers who rose up to speak negative words against Moses. God led these people around in a 12-mile circle until they all died in the wilderness. This came about as a result of their negative words. God listens to what we say. Doubt and unbelief rule the negative heart and are the power and strength of the nay-sayers. All of us must continually work on our attitudes and, through faith, build our character. Our attitudes are a pattern, and character is the result of that pattern over a period of time. Whether it is a good or bad pattern depends on whether the heart is negative or positive.

Before salvation came, oh how sick we all were. Thankfully, with salvation came health and a new vocabulary of faith. A new heart is mandatory if we are to be changed from a sickly minus factor to a healthy plus factor in Christ. If we want a positive, godly character to be developed within us, we must overcome the temptation to be a nay-sayer. By allowing positive attitudes to be firmly set in the heart and become fully operational, we'll show forth the right character attitude. God is pleased with us when we flow in the fruit of His Spirit in this way. Galatians 5:22-23 says, "But the fruit of the Spirit is love, joy, peace, longsuffering, gentleness, goodness, faith, meekness, temperance: against such there is no law." These are the positive character traits we need. We should all desire a character that God can trust and an attitude that won't grieve and offend the Holy Spirit. This kind of character propels us to walk in the likeness of Christ. The key is to be filled with the Spirit and be led by the Spirit. If we walk in our negative flesh, we'll return to speaking negative words that will force us into doubt and unbelief, resulting in a bad character and a wrong attitude that will hinder us from attaining our rightful inheritance in Jesus Christ. (See Galatians 5:17-21.)

To walk in the Spirit and avoid the hidden powers of darkness, it is essential that we speak to God daily, talking to Him first thing in the morning, last thing at night, and all throughout the day. It is not enough just to attend church if we want the kind of faith and spiritual power that has been decreasing in recent years. Many of us have gotten too busy for God, and our spiritual heart is suffering. We are in desperate need of fresh, positive words, more spiritual exercise, and a better diet of worship, prayer, and praise. Rather than feasting on negative words that cause our desires to become more covetous and self-seeking and that bring about our low disposition and self-esteem, we must return to the positive side of Christian living. Yes, we must approach the precious things of God and the things of this world with a clean attitude and a right character, using the character and attitude of Christ as our example. To avoid a negative heart, we must obey 2 Peter 1:5-7, which says, "And beside this, giving all diligence, add to your faith virtue; and to virtue knowledge; and to knowledge temperance; and to temperance patience; and to patience godliness; and to godliness brotherly kindness; and to brotherly kindness charity."

As we seek after God to serve Him and have the victory in His presence, let us also be mindful to carefully maintain a positive heart at all times as we work out our soul's salvation. But, let us remember that what we view positively must stem from agreement with God's Word. Does God always approve of a positive outlook in every situation at all times? Absolutely not. We must not allow ourselves to be deceived and to think positively about issues that are clearly against God's Word. A positive heart that is fully in God's hands by wisdom and understanding exists by the Word of Truth. It agrees with God always and is not affected by the popular opinions of the world. The spirit that rules the negative heart and the Spirit that rules the positive heart will never agree or exist in eternity together. We as believers must always remain vigilant and recognize that satan is the author of the negative, while God is the author of the positive.

TOO MANY "BUT'S" IN THE HOUSE

One Sunday in 1998, I preached a sermon called "There are too many 'But's' in the House." The title of the sermon shocked many people in the pews. In the sermon, I talked about people who are always saying, "I know, but," "I would, but," "Uh-huh, but," and "Yes, but." While we are free moral agents and delivered ambassadors in the Lord, we need to know that where God has received a "Yes, Lord" from our hearts, He never expects a "No" to be formed there again. In other words, God expects us not only to surrender to Him for salvation, but also in all areas of life.

I can't speak for you, but it took years for God to sow enough positive words into my heart to change my life, destiny, and vocabulary. For many who have been plagued by a negative heart, that negativity began at a young age or even while they were in their mother's womb. This is especially true if the mother herself was a negatively bound person with a negative heart. Even unsaved medical doctors are beginning to instruct pregnant mothers regarding the power of attitude, character, and lifestyle. From the womb to adulthood, we are affected by the words spoken by our parents as well as by the attitudes of their hearts. Jesus Christ never used negative words without the positive being in control. In His heart, He is the sure foundation, and He became God's positive Son for us all. Isaiah 28:16 says, "Therefore thus saith the Lord God, Behold, I lay in Zion for a foundation a stone, a tried stone, a precious corner stone, a sure foundation: he that believeth shall not make haste."

A POSITIVE HEART MUST RULE OVER NEGATIVE FLESH

In Christ, we must be sure, positive, certain, and never doubt (see Hebrews 10:23 and James 1:6), but in order to be this way we must know in our hearts what is right, pure, clean, and good in the sight of God. A negative heart produces un-surety, doubt, bewilderment, and confusion. A positive heart, on the other hand, allows us to trust God's promises to us. We all know that we will die one day, but we can be just as sure that the Lord has gone before us to prepare a place for us. We must keep the faith of God and faith in God, for it is our blessed positive assurance for our hearts.

Let us view a very serious truth to gain more understanding. The spiritual heart sits in the midst of the spirit man—our hidden man within us—which is priceless and even more valuable than the natural heart that lies within the natural body. Both are subject to us in all that we do, say, eat, act out, and become involved in. Both the spiritual and natural hearts react to what is available to them, whether it is good, bad, right, or wrong. Positive or negative, the heart will feed, digest, store, and manifest whatever has been sown within it. Just like the brain has power with the natural heart, our will and our desires have power with the spiritual heart. In fact, the heart tends to feed from our will just as much as it does from the mind. A negative spirit is directly linked to insecurity, mental depression, and low self-esteem. Unless there is a serious physical malfunction, these can easily be eliminated by the joy of the Lord and the power of salvation. Our level of faith in God makes the real difference in the end. We need a positive heart to rule over our negative flesh. We can't plant a negative seed within our spiritual heart and expect faith to grow. Without faith, it's impossible to please God, and all that the Lord isn't pleased with in the end He will cast into outer darkness. This is why we must trust in the Lord, the Great Physician, to direct our hearts, minds, and souls, even those tender emotions and feelings that cause most of us to say wrong things without being mindful of the power of the thoughts and emotions.

This is why we must remember that, even though we're saved, we can still believe in a negative position or situation that will cause us loss and hurt. It is also important to recognize that communication is not always verbalized; often we silently speak within our hearts. If the words that are being spoken in our hearts and not through our mouth are believed, they are just as effective as if they were spoken. We say a lot of words in our heart that never come forth out of our mouth (see Deuteronomy 8:17, 18:21; Jeremiah 5:24; 13:22; and Romans. 10:6).

Because our heart's "words" are just as effective as spoken words, the Lord judges us by the motives and intents of our hearts, which include our thoughts and imaginations. Our thoughts are usually manifested through our flesh. Therefore, we should be careful not to speak negatively while also being very careful not to *think* negative thoughts. Negative thoughts such as "No, I don't believe," "No, I won't obey church rules or regulations," and "No, I don't think my marriage is going to last" all have very serious ramifications. These all negate the power of unity and the prayer of faith. When we pray for a needed change due to an existing problem, faith words must continually be spoken in conjunction with the words we use to ask the Lord for what we need. Negative words (that aren't intended to produce a positive result) never get through to the heart of God. He is "negative immune." Unfortunately, though, people are not immune to negativity. This makes negative words extremely powerful, dangerous, and deceitful. If negative power remains active within any church, there can never be strong unity, nor will there be the manifestation of the Holy Spirit of God as there should be.

CONSEQUENCES OF A NEGATIVE HEART

Why are pastors dying at a young age, retiring from preaching the gospel early, or even stepping down from a position of leadership never to return? I believe it's because they have negative, slothful hearts that murmur and complain loudly, saying, "I can't," "I'm not able," "No," "Not right now," and "Get somebody else to do that" rather than "If it be God's will," "Let God's will be done," "I'll pray about it," "I'm not too sure, but what does the Bible say about it?" and other positive phrases. The church, the gospel, salvation, and life itself is set up and operated by the Lord. When nations, governments, and any other systems don't accept

99

God's way, they won't work properly. The end will surely be defeat, a Code Blue disaster, or a Code Red woe. Church, if we desire a positive heart that will please God, there has to be a change of vocabulary for us all. This change can only manifest itself as a result of true biblical salvation.

As a pastor for these past 16 years, I have observed heated arguments, intense anger, destroying utterances, and division within the church. These things also occur in (supposedly) good Christian homes where love is absent, peace seems to be on vacation, and joy is seldom seen. The more we allow faithless, negative words to infiltrate our lives, the weaker our walk with the Lord will be. I have also observed many people who seem to have been called long before their time as a result of negative hearts. I believe that if the medical world would get involved with biblical faith, doctors would teach their patients to be positive and speak more positive words. As a result, I believe miracles of healings, deliverances, and blessings would take place. If every hospital would set forth protective, positive guidelines for the spiritual heart as well as they do the natural heart we would see a massive decline in abortion, health care cost, sickness, and disease. A positive spiritual heart has a profound effect upon our longevity.

POSITIVE IS RIGHT; NEGATIVE IS WRONG

There is a battle that rages between good and evil and right and wrong in everyone's life. Therefore, we must begin to monitor both our natural life and our spiritual life, for all that we allow to become real and rule in our lives will eventually determine our end result. Walking in the Spirit requires daily commitment. That is why we must continually "check up" on the state of our hearts. Luke 6:45 says, "A good man out of the good treasure of his heart bringeth forth that which is good; and an evil man out of the evil treasure of his heart bringeth forth that which is evil: for of the abundance of the heart his mouth speaketh." If we want good to win over evil in our lives, we must ensure that our heart is positive.

The power of wrong has increased to the point that very few people seem to even know what is right. For instance, I know of a man who walked around daily with his wedding band on the wrong finger. One day someone noticed it and touched his shoulder saying "Sir, did you know that you have your wedding band on the wrong finger?" "Yes, I know;" he replied, "I married the wrong woman!" The man's inner heart's wrong was reflected outwardly, and wrong seemed right to him. The more positive the heart, the more love, peace, and joy it will hold. In Proverbs 23:7, the Bible encourages us to become fully aware of the inner life of the heart, to know our thoughts, mind, soul and emotions.

Thoughts are exposed and expressed by deeds and spoken words, which shape our tomorrows. Words or deeds that come forth from negative thoughts must be guarded, for spoken words of "yes" to God or "no" to God are what have us standing in the place where we are today. This is why it is so important to observe Proverbs 4:23, which says, "Keep thy heart with all diligence; for out of it are the issues of life." This verse instructs us about the seriousness of what we believe in our hearts. (See also Matthew 12:34.) The Bible also gives us a great way to counteract the negative heart when it begins to utter too many words that are displeasing to God and man. We can simply put our hands *over our mouth* to still and hush the negative heart.

Proverbs 30:32 says, "If thou hast done foolishly in lifting up thyself, or if thou hast thought evil, lay thine hand upon thy mouth." (See also Judges 18:19; Job 40:4, 21:5, and 29:9-10; Psalm 55:21, 59:12, and 62:4; Proverbs 6:2-12 and 13:3; Micah 7:16; James 3:10; Revelations 9:19; and Titus 1:11.)

God's Word in our mouth, flowing from a positive heart, will always, in every case, make us and mold us into better persons in the sight of God. We want to be all that we can be. It must be noted again and again that as Christ went to that old rugged cross, and, as He hung there, He never spoke negative utterances (as most of us would have spoken if we were innocently giving our lives for those who were guilty) such as "Oh no," "Not I," "I can't," "Why me?" "Not now, Father," or "I won't." Rather, he showed us the better way. He was silent, holding to a positive attitude, saying, "Father, not my will, but thine be done!" He was and is the perfect example for us when worry, fear, grief, and the storms of life overtake us and we don't know what to do or which way to turn. Even a saved, negative heart in the midst of serious warfare, without proper guidance may utter, "I don't know how, Lord," "Why me, Lord?" "No, this just can't be," and "Why is this happening to me?" But when we try to follow the example of Jesus, we can turn these negative words into positive ones.

When floods of ungodly thoughts and words rise to consume, kill, or destroy, we must walk by faith, say what God says and utter according to scripture the desired positive result. By doing this, we redirect and reset our heart into the positive and realign it with God's will, and the end result will be the best that it can possibly be. God's will for all of us is 100 percent positive; however, it's in our hands to maintain a perfect, pure, and clean positive heart. If we do this we can enjoy some of heaven's great benefits right here on earth.

THE NEGATIVE HEART IS CODE BLUE TO YOU

Let's look at a Code Blue tare that encompassed both the negative and the positive. This is the tare of "Not," that supports its leader "No," "Have not," "Will not," "Could not," "Do not," "Is not," and "Shall not." These indicate that something could have been or should have been—but wasn't. These are particles of negation that express the idea of no, implying some type of refusal. Once the heart becomes fully experienced in the "not" voice, it may say "no" when the answer should be "yes." Your heart will tell you that it will never be, when God has ordained it "to be" in your life. The "not's" always breed insecurity in our spirit man, and an insecure heart can never be fully trusted. God's voice always remains in the positive. Even when He says "no," it is a positive statement and not a negative utterance of His heart. But beware when the devil or your flesh tells you "yes," because it's still a negative. How can this be? Satan never does the will of God or involves his wicked heart to obey; therefore, all of his works, words, and will are Code Blue negatives. When he says "yes" by your flesh or his spirit, it's really a "no." The results that will manifest will certainly be negative. "No" is an awesome word when we speak it against God's will or purpose. When He returns to this earth in His wrath, anger, and fiery-destroying power, many "no's" will certainly be heard in the earth realm, especially the "oh no's!"

We all have instances in which we have said "yes" to satan and "no" to God. At the age of 18, I said "yes" to sexual activity, and at the age of 23 I first said "yes" to alcohol and drugs. My "yes" response to these things turned my heart around into a negative position against God's will for my life. What we may see as a temporary benefit may produce a lifetime of negative results. Therefore, let us say "yes" to God, "amen" to His will forever, and let us obey His Word from the rising and the setting of the sun. Let our soul say "yes" and our mind say "Lord, thy will be done." A negative heart toward God is Code Blue to you. The right attitude in our daily walk with Christ, however, will allow us to be set forth and perfected as well as Christ develops our character. Good character and a right attitude make our God happy with us and eager to respond to our needs. Jeremiah 17:9-10 tells us that the "heart is deceitful above all things and desperately wicked." Because of this, what we see isn't always what we get, what we want isn't always what we need, and what we say isn't always what should be said. If we're to enter the full realm of the eternal to enjoy the fruits of our divine destiny, we must rid ourselves of the negative and encompass the fullness of the positive. For in Jesus Christ, there must only be "yea" and "amen."

7

SPEAK TO MY HEART, LORD

The requirement for hearing and obeying God's voice is that we must believe from our hearts. Moses explained to Israel that when we sin the Lord becomes angry, if we repent and obey His voice, all will be well (Deuteronomy 4:27-36, 5:22-33). It's a matter of God speaking to our hearts while we have a willing heart to hear and obey; for the Lord never speaks in vain or speaks words of vanity. Obedience to the voice of God is a must. The voice of God protects and soothes our fears, brings peace and eases our troubled minds and calms vexed souls and worried hearts.

God desires to speak to us about everything that concerns us, both naturally and spiritually. God has the answer to all complex questions, unbearable circumstances, and problems that are beyond our control. We need to hear what God has to say in order to do His perfect will—Oh speak to my heart Lord, tell me what you see! (2 Chronicles 16:9).

WHY DON'T WE HEAR FROM GOD?

Today, let the cry of the righteous go forth unto the Lord of Hosts saying, "Lord, here I am; speak to my heart!" More than 28 times in the New Testament, Jesus Christ said, "Let He that have ears to hear, let him hear." We must be willing to hear what God is saying to us if we truly want the Lord to speak to us.

In God's quest to transform the hidden man of the heart (see 1 Peter 3:4) to be like His Son Jesus Christ, He begins to remove every obstacle that interferes with this process. This is sometimes a long, painful process as God begins to remove destructive heart

105

habits, reveal selfish heart motives, and strip away impure heart emotions. All of these vices stop up the ears of the heart. Healing and reconstructive surgery have to take place in order to hear a word from the Lord. Our heart must undergo a renewal process, during which old walls have to be torn down and new walls erected. Child of God, God has a word for you today. You don't have to wait until a prophet comes to town, you can hear Him for yourself. He is able to speak to your heart. You just have to be willing to listen to what He has to say.

LORD, WE NEED TO HEAR FROM YOU

Because of weak-hearted leaders, we have pastors who should still be deacons and apostles who are actually evangelists. Why am I being so hard on the church structure? Because many souls are being deceived, and God is not pleased. Do we really want God to speak the truth to our hearts? What would He say? Would he tell us to take the offering money and give to the poor rather than spend it on our grand buildings and ourselves? Would He instruct us to take someone less fortunate than ourselves shopping to meet their needs? Would He ask us to come up higher in himself? Beloved, God's thoughts are unlike any we have heard, and our hearts must be fine-tuned to hear a word from the Lord.

Our heart is God's sanctuary and His kingdom. Our body is the temple, and He has the right to speak within us, to us, and through us. In Old Testament times, God spoke to Moses, and Moses spoke to the people. In Jesus' time, God's only Son spoke to His disciples and the people on God's behalf; however, at the Cross, that system ended also. When Pentecost had fully come, the Holy Spirit entered *man's heart* and set up the final system upon the earth by which we communicate with God. This system will remain until the return of Christ.

One day, I went to visit a very large church near my home. As I drove up to the church, I could hardly find a parking space, for the lot was filled with great expensive cars. I noticed the pastor's Rolls Royce and his wife's Mercedes, and I was happy for their blessings. The church was packed with people. The floors were spotless. The pews were so soft that I sank down three inches when I sat down. The people wore lavish, beautiful clothing. The pastor preached until his robe was soaking wet with sweat. Then a still quiet voice spoke to my heart saying, "*Go from this filthy place of iniquity and return not again unto it!*" I looked around me quickly thinking that it was someone joking with me, but there was no one. As I glanced at the chandeliers that looked like they were worth a fortune, the Lord placed a scripture in my mind from 1 Samuel 16: 7, "Man looketh on the outward appearance, but the Lord looketh on the heart." God had spoken to me! I understood what He was saying, that man builds million dollar churches and material goods such as automobiles and houses and things, but God builds priceless hearts. It does no good to own a million dollar home and have a ten dollar heart.

What surprised me as I left the church was that God, knowing my heart and the heart of that local assembly, warned me to flee! Nevertheless, in ignorance, I spoke back to God, saying, "But Lord, you've blessed them so much—look at the sanctuary; look at the stylish clothes and cars!" God said in reply, "*I am indeed a God who blesses. Even the most wicked of all men, I have still blessed. But, you must obey me!*" Immediately I began to pray silently in the spirit for the hearts of the leaders and the people of that church, that God would be able to speak a heart-changing word to them. Then God spoke again, and I heard him clearly say that "*Even in this house, My Word is preached, and yet few have a right heart in my sight to even hear the one who's doing the preaching.*" Now I understand, and I speak to the Body of Christ that no one should assume that his heart is right just because he is a member of a church that preaches and teaches the Word of God. Material possessions don't determine the value of a heart, and a good sermon is not necessarily the evidence of God's presence (See Matthew 3:15-23).

God has to be able to communicate to our hearts, for He alone and none other knows its true condition. This is why I now believe that, regardless of the title given to a man, every minister of the gospel must consider himself to be a prime candidate for a new heart.

CHURCH ORDER IS ACHIEVED ONLY IF WE HEAR AND OBEY THE VOICE OF GOD

Jeremiah 13:10 says, "This evil people, which refuse to hear my words, which walk in the imagination of their heart, and walk after other gods, to serve them, and to worship them, shall even be as this girdle, which is good for nothing."

In the modern day church in which the hearts of people have not been given to God, man is in control and the Spirit of God is bound in fetters and chains. We have deemed certain areas in the church building to be more holy than other areas; however, God resides in the heart of man, and our bodies are His sanctuary and His temple. What can be more holy than where the Spirit of God abides? Today, the heart of every believer must be set aside for God, for the mouth speaks and the mind thinks from within the depths of the heart.

Far too many preachers preach great sermons about love, faith, and prosperity without considering the heart conditions of the people. Many speak from their own knowledge and under-standing and not from the heart of God. I am a firm believer that if God's heart were preached in our morning and evening wor-ship services, many would be turned from unrighteousness back to righteousness. We must deal with the hearts of the people, much like Jesus dealt with the heart of the woman at the well in John 4:5-30.

The heart is the seeding ground for the Word of God (Matthew 13:1-18). God's voice and His word are specifically heart-designed. If a heart isn't firmly planted in God's hands, it will most likely not recognize, and therefore reject, the Word of God. For the past several years, there has been an increasing number of people who have called me up to ask, "Do you have a word from the Lord for me that I may be blessed?" I always say, "Yes, there is a word from the Lord and it is this—get your heart right with God!" The teaching of true blessings has been out of order for many years and desperately needs to be corrected. (See my book *Jael, Blessed Above Women* by Xulon Press for more about this topic.) The desires of our heart have become out of focus with the will of God for our lives. We must hear God's voice and obey His will if we are to meet His divine purpose. Only then will we recognize God's voice speaking to our hearts.

Jeremiah 7:23 says, "But this thing commanded I them, saying, Obey my voice, and I will be your God, and ye shall be my people: and walk ye in all the ways that I have commanded you, that it may be well unto you." (See also Deuteronomy 27:10; 1 Samuel 12:14-15 and 15:19-22; Jeremiah 11:4-7, 26:13, and 38:20; Daniel 9:11; and Zechariah 6:15.) We cannot obey that which we cannot hear. Without open hearts, we will miss what God is saying to us in our spirit and through His Word. When we study the Scriptures, God is there speaking to our hearts. There is order, safety, great benefits, and life in hearing and obeying the voice of God.

Remember, we must be inwardly qualified for God's approval. If we are not heart-approved, we will not hear his voice to fulfill His will or be used for His purpose.

WHAT IS THAT SOUND?

We benefit greatly when we listen continually to God's voice. What we hear and deem to be from God is based on the condition of our heart. In other words, if my heart is steeped in greed or stinginess, I will never obey the voice that instructs me to give tithes and offerings. Often, we attribute God's voice to the voice of satan. As we begin to bind up satan, we miss the fact that God is trying to bless us! In Genesis 22:1-17, God told Abraham to kill his only son. Abraham had practiced hearing the voice of God, so he did not dismiss this strange request, despite the fact that God had never made a request like this before. (Most of us, if not all of us, would have mistakenly attributed this to the voice of satan.) Abraham heard and obeyed in his heart, and God blessed him for his obedience. Just as he was about to kill his son, the Angel of the Lord stopped him and commended him on his obedience and love toward God. Had Abraham ignored the voice of God, who knows what might have happened?

The Bible is full of illustrations regarding the importance of listening to the voice of God. For instance, the 12 disciples were set for greatness because they listened to Jesus and tried to do His will and obey His words. But what if they didn't hear? Where would we be? Faith that moves mountains comes from hearing God's voice (Romans 10:17).

When we refuse to listen to the voice of Jesus Christ, or don't consult Him for serious answers, we can expect delays and trouble. We read and study the Bible to know God's Word. Obeying God's Word reveals how much we love Him, and His Word to us—words of wisdom, knowledge, warnings, and under-standing—show how much He loves us. We must hear His voice and not allow our hearts to become hardened and blind and our ears to become dull of hearing (Matthew 13:15; Hebrews 5:11). I remember the time I had just purchased a new Lincoln Town car and was driving along the highway at a high rate of speed. A small voice spoke to my heart saying, "*Don, slow down, you are going too fast, you're going to get pulled over by the state police.*" I didn't listen. The voice came a second time saying, "*Don, you're breaking the law; Christians should obey the law of the land, even help to establish the law. You must slow down.*" The moment I slowed down to the speed limit and came up over a hill, there were four police cars with radar detectors to catch speeding lawbreakers. The Lord spoke to me saying, "*Don, see, you must listen to me.*" I asked God to forgive me, for it is not the police whom we as believers need to worry about so much; it's God. I thanked the Lord for His warning voice, the same voice that warned the prophets of impending danger. God doesn't always speak to His prophets, pastors, and teachers in an audible voice, but He often speaks to their hearts.

God is our guide, our Great Shepherd, and our life's heart physician, who operates within our lifestyle telling us when to hold, when to fold, when to walk away, and when to run. He calls us by name (Psalm 85:8; John 10:1-8). The whole Bible holds the basic intents of God's heart and the contents of His divine will.

God speaks through His Word, through interpretation of tongues, and by revelation, wisdom, and knowledge to connect with His people. He speaks to us in our prayer time as we pray without ceasing. Prayer is two-fold; we speak to God, and He speaks back unto us. This is true holy communion. Many times the Lord also gets our attention (if we're listening) through preaching, teaching, or a personal word from a fellow believer. When He speaks, He is still surprised when we don't hear and obey Him. He sometimes goes one step further and speaks to us through visions and dreams. Numbers 12:6 says, "And he said, Hear now my words: If there be a prophet among you, I the Lord will make myself known unto him in a vision, and will speak unto him in a dream." (See Acts 9:10-12.)

Not only does God desire to speak to us, He also watches over us. We sing the song that says "His eyes are on the sparrow, and I know He watches me!" What God is really looking for is a pure and perfect heart that will do His will and be used for His purpose. 2 Chronicles 16:9 says, "For the eyes of the Lord run to and from throughout the whole earth, to show himself strong in the behalf of them whose heart is perfect toward him."

Why is it so hard for us to hear God's voice? In Mark 4:39, Jesus speaks to the wind and the sea, ordering them to be still. If the wind and sea heard His voice and obeyed, why can't we? Most of God's people never consider just how long God has patiently waited and how much He has longed to talk to them heart to heart. When we were lost sinners, satan used our vocal chords, our bodies, and our minds to do his evil will, causing us to curse, swear, lie, deceive, and commit many sins. These things were all grievous to God. But thanks be to Christ and His atoning sacrifice, we now speak a powerful new vocabulary, and we are able to hear a new voice if we will listen. This is possible because we have a new life and a new heart.

In these evil, last days, believers must stay connected to God, pay close attention to what the Lord is saying, and fast and pray without ceasing, saying, "Lord, speak now to my heart!" It is wise to fast for days unto the Lord until His voice rings clear. The

Lord makes many attempts to get through to our emotions, consciousness, feelings, mind, and flesh using various methods:

- He speaks from heaven above;
- He speaks from within us;
- He speaks through His servants;
- He speaks through Christ;
- He speaks by His Word;
- He speaks by His Spirit; and,
- He speaks to our hearts.

GOD, WHAT ARE YOU SAYING?

God always has something good to say, even if we feel it is bad. He often uses circumstances to speak to us as well. In every bad situation, things could be worse. Even if a person should lose his home, car, job, or mate, God still speaks. For one thing, that person can be thankful to still be alive. In all things we are able to give thanks. When we have thankful hearts despite negative circumstances, we are in essence saying, "God, I'm still listening, and I still trust You!" Because so many have refused to listen to Jesus, millions have perished before their time. Satan speaks to us when we're vulnerable, but the more we listen to Jesus, the less satan has the power to speak in our lives. The more God's Word becomes alive in our hearts, the weaker satan becomes. Although he comes to steal the word that's sown by the Holy Spirit in our heart, he loses his power if we listen for God's voice.

Matthew 13:1-28 outlines conditions of various hearts in which God attempts to sow His Word. Therefore, we must, as spiritual farmers, make sure that the ground of our hearts is properly cultivated and fully prepared for God's seeds are faith, love, truth, knowledge, the spoken and written Word, and peace. Having these power seeds sown within a pure and clean heart, the heart becomes easily receptive to God's voice. Therefore, the key to hearing the voice of God is to maintain a good seeded heart through continual prayer and a firm commitment of obedience to

His voice. Yes, the heart can be good if we allow God to make it good! (See Luke 8:15.)

Heard daily, God's Word acts as a seal and protectant for new seeds of faith sown within us. God speaks His word in us, to us, and through us so that our hearts will not become as hard as stone and not able to receive what the Lord has for us. We must listen or risk becoming lukewarm in our walk with Christ. Revelation 3:15-16 says, "I know thy works, that thou art neither cold nor hot: I would thou wert cold or hot. So then because thou art lukewarm, and neither cold nor hot, I will spue thee out of my mouth." This fate can be prevented if we remain receptive to God's written and spoken Word.

God knows our heart's attitude as well as its intents and contents. Therefore, He knows when to speak, how long to speak, and when to stop speaking. It's time for the Body of Christ to once again turn their hearts toward seeking and serveing the true and living God with all their might. This requires the willingness to hear His voice and obey His will. We must remember that the purer the heart is, the easier the voice of the Lord can be heard. A defiled, diseased, sick, or unsaved heart has very little power to hear the voice of God. It was God's voice that produced His Word. His voice is all that His Word will ever be and all that you and I can ever become in Christ Jesus. His voice speaks new things into existence that never were—without His voice, they would have never been (John 21:25).

So, if God's voice is speaking to us, what then is the problem? The conflict lies between the natural man (the flesh) and the spirit man. Each has a voice, and they often speak at the same time. When the spirit man speaks, what is the natural man saying, and vice versa? The heart can speak, the flesh man can utter its voice, and the soul can cry out. But which voice can we truly trust? This will be a dilemma for us unless we, as true believers, follow the leading of the Holy Spirit. While we know our flesh man well, we need to know much more about our spirit man and our own heart. From birth we walked, fed, and existed in the natural man, leaving our spirit man to die as it sat in darkness. Then the light of salvation brought our spirit man to life, giving it full functioning powers and a new heart. As new creatures walking in the spirit of holiness, having been born again, we must also speak a new language and be spoken to in a new way.

In my opinion, this includes speaking in tongues, which allows the spirit man to communicate with God in a way that the natural man cannot. As an American I do appreciate the English language, but I know that God's mouth is not as man's mouth, His language is not as man's language, and His understanding is not as man's understanding. Therefore, I speak God's language and also the English language. Both are very beneficial. While the flesh man is still with us, he has no more authority over us if we are saved. The flesh and the spirit coexist in one body. The flesh man must perish daily while the spirit man gains predominance. And of course, it is the spirit man who will be alive forevermore (1 Corinthians 2:12-15).

When we face a Code Red or Code Blue problem or circumstance, what must we do? We must listen for God's voice as He speaks to our hearts. When we say what the Word says with obedience, cast down every negative thought and imagination, bind and take authority over the thing sent to us from the enemy, and guard our heart, there will be no weapon that's formed against us that shall prosper.

8

You Must Have Heart

Deuteronomy 20:2-4: *"And it shall be, when ye are come nigh unto the battle, that the priest shall approach and speak unto the people, And shall say unto them, Hear, O Israel, ye approach this day unto battle against your enemies: let not your hearts faint, fear not, and do not tremble, neither be ye terrified because of them; For the Lord your God is He that goeth with you, to fight for you against your enemies, to save you."*

In the midst of greed, poor choices, and bad decisions by many modern churches and religious organizations, the heart of man is guilty. Many are still unlearned regarding ways to spiritually obtain holy and righteous hearts. Because of this, spiritual hearts are weak, people are ceasing to walk by faith, and few are showing forth God's true love and salvation from the heart. The church has lost its hunger to see miracles and its desire for the blind to see, the deaf to hear, and the dead to be raised to life. There's no heart in today's ministry to lay hands on the sick, cast out devils, and speak with new tongues. Just like many who have come before us, we have become lax, unlearned in spiritual matters, and oblivious to the real presence of Jesus Christ in the midst of our services. Where are the holy mothers who fasted 40 days and nights and were able to bring godly correction to the saints? Sometimes, their mere presence as they walked up and down the aisles of the church would bring godly conviction and anointing. Where are the righteous fathers who prayed without ceasing and established their homes by the Word of God? By and large, Christians no longer have the heart to fast and pray without ceasing, nor do they continue daily in the Word of God and the gospel of Jesus Christ. We are losing heart.

Because there's no real heart for the fullness of God's presence, there are believers who lust after money, power, material gain, sexual gratification, and other matters rooted in the flesh. These believers want to receive a blessing rather than be a blessing. In fact, one of the most needed scripture verses, Acts 20:35, is one that is not emphasized nearly enough. This verse states, "It is more blessed to give than to receive." Lord, we need heart!

We continue to lose heart at an alarming rate. Believers all over the world are losing heart for fasting, total commitment, a daily diet of the Word, and the responsibility that comes with a relationship with God. Go to the local bookstores, schools or colleges and it will be difficult to find a book on the spiritual heart because books ranging from the topics of sex and the occult to real estate and business have top priority. Unfortunately, the problem extends to the modern family home, where it is evident that humans are no longer involved in becoming familiar with their own hearts. Sadly, we are learned in every area of society except in the subject of our spiritual heart. Yet, heart knowledge is what we need the most!

Spiritual heart training and teaching programs should be the most important programs presented in our churches, regardless of affiliation or doctrine. I believe that if those who are bound by false religions and doctrines knew their true heart condition, destiny, and end result, they would repent and turn to Jesus Christ for help. Jesus Christ, the Son of the living God, wants to dwell in our hearts, which makes the heart the most precious element and power in the whole earth. In fact, I believe it is God's will that the local church become heart training centers. We need better hearts, new hearts, pure hearts, and clean hearts.

"Spiritual teachers" are teaching many ways in which to receive things from God. Financial prosperity teaching is at an all-time high, but have these so-called teachers ever considered that the state of the heart is what determines true prosperity? If not, they are in great error. No goal, prosperity plan, purpose, or idea should be more important than having a right heart that is pleasing to God. In fact, the richest person in the world—one who is the most blessed—is that person who walks before God with a pure and clean heart. We're commanded to walk by faith, and faith can only spring from a right heart. Whether we experience victory, success, failure, or defeat in Code Blue situations depends almost entirely upon the condition of the heart. Many have achieved much natural success and wealth but are bound by the poverty of their spiritual hearts. Outward success doesn't assure us of inward wealth. In fact, nearly all of the valuable things that we can see with the naked eye—such as diamonds, rare paintings, gold, and money—cannot benefit our spirit man spiritually or eternally. Financial security is false; it is temporary shelter without eternal benefits and is easily destroyed in a moment.

The Church, the Body of Christ, needs more heart information and heart revelation from the Lord. We have the revelation of Scripture, but there is an emergency need for a revelation of the heart. If we just ask Him, God will never hold anything back from a willing heart. God's Word is the best heart information book available for the believer. Being properly heart informed through God's Word will keep many from Code Blue attacks.

Mankind has spent billions of dollars learning about the physical human body, this universe, the moon, and the stars but has spent very little to learn about man's most precious commodity—the spiritual heart. Just as medical heart specialists spend much of their lives researching the natural heart, so should every spiritual leader, fervently seek more information and revelation on the spiritual heart. If spiritual leaders would do this, God would enable them to be spiritual heart specialists capable of effectively ministering to God's people. In a perfect world—one in which secular physicians recognized the ultimate truth about the heart—we would see medical doctors from local hospitals sitting in the church pews to learn about the awesome spiritual heart from the teachings of church pastors.

But "spiritual heart specialists" are not the only ones privy to the truths that God gives us regarding our hearts. Heart information is obtained by daily opening our hearts to faith, love, and God's Word and by living holy, set-apart lives as we seek God with all of our heart and soul. Heart prayers, heart praises and worship, and heart commitment are also a must. Rightly divided, the Word of God reveals, molds, and preserves the heart of the believer. Since God works through man, it's very crucial that Bible teachers be free to release any new heart information and revelation that God makes available to the Body of Christ.

WE NEED HEART FELLOWSHIP

Right fellowship with God and man encourages and strengthens the heart. However, if the heart isn't set, focused, or firmly committed, the heart may faint. This causes fellowship to cease. Even a great ministry that is fully ordained of God will sadly cease if it persists in a Code Red State. That's why it is essential that the heart condition of individuals be carefully examined before any church fellowship, services, or the merging of religious organization takes place. To fellowship with God or man, there must be intimate heart-to-heart communication. If one does not have a right heart, his brethren will soon seem to be his enemy. Hostility, foolishness, confusion, and disunity will soon be in the midst.

HEART FAILURE

1 Samuel 17:32 says, "And David said to Saul, Let no man's heart fail because of him [Goliath], thy servant will go and fight with this Philistine." (See also Genesis 42:28 and Psalm 40:12.) David gives us a good example here of the importance of setting one's heart before God even when the hearts of others are failing them.

To succeed in your calling, you must set your heart to that which God has called you to do. The error some people make in not setting their heart has caused many heart failures in ministry. The heart can be set by the spoken word, confession of faith, and obedience to God's Word. I remember growing up in a house where the roof would leak whenever it rained. We placed buckets, pans, and jars underneath the leaks to catch the water and prevent damage to our valuables. A leaky heart is just like a leaky house—it will cause damage to the valuables housed inside the hearts such as faith, love, joy, and peace. Spiritual heart failure is a serious matter of the heart.

Heart failure is one of the most dreaded and serious events that can take place in the natural or spiritual body. It's the prime reason that the Code Red warning exists. Heart failure doesn't automatically mean death, but in most cases, it signifies that the heart has failed to produce strength, power, or the functions necessary for that person to go forth or continue on as they were. When David faced the giant Goliath, I believe that he gave us one of the most valuable lessons on the heart found in Scripture. 1 Samuel 17:32-35: "And David said to Saul, Let no man's heart fail because of him; thy servant will go and fight with this Philistine. And Saul said to David, Thou art not able to go against this Philistine to fight with him: for thou art but a youth, and he a man of war from his youth. And David said unto Saul, Thy servant kept his father's sheep, and there came a lion, and a bear, and took a lamb out of the flock: And I went out after him, and smote him, and delivered it out of his mouth: and when he arose against me, I caught him by his beard, and smote him, and slew him."

Due to heart failure caused by fear, neither Saul nor the children of Israel had the heart to go against Goliath and be victorious. It is the heart of the believer who is in right standing with God that can face overwhelming odds and come out victorious! Christ addressed His disciples saying, "Fear not." Spiritual heart failure, caused by fear, robs us of the victory that is waiting for us when we trust and obey.

Can it be possible that the Tin Man character, in the story book tales of *The Wizard of Oz*, revealed to the whole Christian community the one thing we should desire the most—to have a heart? Today, there are hundreds of leaders holding high offices within in the church and charging the church a high yearly fee, and all the while they have no heart. To avoid the *"no heart"* problem, God has promised His people that he will give them a heart to know Him, even a new heart and that He would be their God. Jeremiah 24:7 says, "And I will give them a heart to know Me, that I am the Lord: and they shall be my people, and I will be their God: for they shall return unto me with their whole heart." (See also Ezekiel 19-21 and 36:26-29.)

PROTECTION FROM FAINTING SPELLS OF THE HEART

Prayer strengthens the complete structure of the heart. Luke 18:1 says, "And He [Jesus] spake a parable unto them to this end, that men ought always to pray, and not to faint." Faith keeps the heart pure; love binds the heart and seals it in Christ; and prayer strengthens the heart so that it will not faint. Faith, love, and prayer allow the heart to function properly. Many times the heart may not fail, but it can become faint. Why? We have a natural man of the flesh and a spiritual man of the spirit. We may daily walk uprightly in the flesh while going about our duties, but that doesn't mean that we haven't fainted in the spirit and that we aren't in need of a heart operation, restoration, or a spiritual heart transplant. When the heart becomes shocked or vexed above measure by grief, frightful news, heated circumstances, or trouble, faintness happens, and we run the risk of losing heart. We faint, especially if we're not God-focused. All over the world, fainting spells occur in the spirit man, and they have caused a great falling away from God and the church. Many have revolted and will never return because of a faint heart. This is a serious heart matter because the day of the Lord is at hand! (See Isaiah 1:4-5.)

A fainting heart is also the sign of a sluggish heart that is without strength. Fainting signals us that the heart is weak, feeble, without enthusiasm, indistinct, and far from certain. We faint when we lose courage and when there seems to be no hope. If there's no heart, then there is no protection when wars, trials, storms, and stumbling blocks are in front of us. How can we succeed in Christ when lust wars against the soul; doubt and unbelief war against faith; flesh wars against the spirit; and the heart wars against the Word of God? The heart must be fed, full, and properly informed. Spiritual fainting spells will cause us to fall backward, become useless, and fall prey to old sins.

Therefore, to avoid spiritual fainting spells, it is imperative that we walk in the spirit and not in the flesh. Our flesh does not retain the Word of God, neither does it ever desire to serve God. We cannot have heart if we are walking solely in the fleshly realm. (See Genesis 42:28 and 45:6; Leviticus 26:36; Ezekiel 21:7-15; Luke 21:25-26; and Galatians 6:8-9 for more on this idea.)

SPIRITUAL HEARTS PRONE TO FAINTING SPELLS

Society's problems—fleshly sins and sicknesses, lust, stress, and personal goals—all tend to wear down the heart's strength. Things like fear and grief or the abnormal or unexpected death of a loved one may also cause faintness of heart. Fainting spells may be temporary, and one can easily recover, but a spiritual heart attack is much more serious and may cause permanent damage. In both cases the victim may never return to church or walk again with God (see John 6:66).

Heart types commonly found in some fainting Christians are fearful hearts, sad hearts, broken hearts, wounded hearts, failed hearts, hard hearts, froward hearts, proud hearts, grieving hearts, and haughty hearts. If the fainting spells are not overcome or corrected, the heart will digress in its Christian power and we become susceptible to Code Red. We become unsure, church chasers, unstable, doubting, and fearful in our walk, drifting along as a ship without an anchor or like a boat without a sail. Faint-heartedness is the final step before a spiritual stroke or heart attack and leads to Code Blue sin and unrighteousness. We cease to be a witness, and our heart isn't involved with God, His promises, or His provisions. We develop a leaky heart in which there's no Word retention or faith. When this happens, a spiritual heart crisis takes place in which the Lord, our Heart Physician, comes to perform a heart transplant or spiritual bypass surgery (Proverbs 23:19). When this happens, the words of Isaiah 40:28-31 give us hope for the cure for a fainting heart: "Hast thou not known? Hast thou not heard, that the everlasting God, the Lord, the Creator of the ends of the earth, fainteth not, neither is weary? there is no searching of his understanding. He giveth power to the faint; and to them that have no might he increaseth strength. Even the youths shall faint and be weary, and the young men shall utterly fall: But they that wait upon the Lord shall renew their strength; they shall mount up with wings as eagles; they shall run, and not be weary; and they shall walk, and not faint" (see also Jeremiah 8:18).

HEART LOSS

We must have heart and not lose heart if we are to keep the faith required in Christ. We must learn what faith can do and benefit from the components that make our faith all that it is. Without these faith components active within the heart, we will surely lose heart. Heart loss of any type is serious. God works to improve our hearts by increasing our faith. The components of faith that give us heart are hope, trust, confidence, courage, and believing. (Study Hebrews 6:11-19; 1 John 3:3, 2:28, and 5:14; 1 Timothy 4:10; Hebrews 2:13 and 3:6-14; Deuteronomy 31:6-23; Psalm 31:24; Matthew 21:22; and John 20:27-31.)

These components of faith act as non-breakable cords that ensure our having enough heart strength to face and defeat the wiles of the devil. We see in Galatians 5:6 that faith works by love. Love is also made up of components that stand as a foundation for every Christian who will love God and man from the heart. Through these mighty elements of love and faith, we can clearly see that we are to remain in love with Christ and walk by faith from a pure and clean heart. A pure heart is not prone to fainting spells when faith is active. Why? God uses faith to purify the heart (see Acts 15:8-9).

A SOUND HEART

Believers must return to holiness and righteousness while giving God high praise and worship with a sound heart. A sound heart is a great defense against temptation, lust, doubt, and Code Red fear. We need a sound heart to avoid spiritual fainting spells. The psalmist reinforces this idea in Psalm 119:80: "Let my heart be sound in thy statutes; that I be not ashamed."

One weapon that makes the heart of man unsound is greed. Greed must never be allowed to seed in the heart. It's a spiritual vampire, a destroying element of bondage. It's a beast that is never satisfied. Many unsound hearts are filled with greed and need to be filled with the Holy Spirit. A greedy heart causes loss of spiritual vision, purpose, and value.

A SET HEART FOR REVIVAL

Most church revivals today are not God-designed or Holy Spirit inspired. The purpose for revivals, concerts, and holy convocations today seems to be to raise funds, ordain church clergy, and see who can dance and praise God for the longest time. Most certainly, these things all have their proper place, but what does it benefit the heart of the people? In the end, what does the revival accomplish? A successful revival isn't predicated upon how much money is raised or how many people attend, but on how many hearts have been changed. Revival the way God ordains it to be must be a time in which all present their heart problems openly unto Him, communing with God continually and intimately for several days and nights for the sole purpose of receiving a better heart, a delivered heart, and a new heart from God. During the season of revival, we should become intimate with God so that our hearts will inform us if there are any heart troubles or malfunctions previously unknown. Revival is a wonderful time to have communion with God's heart and the hearts of church brethren. We need heart if we're to have a successful revival (Ecclesiastes 1:16).

For a successful revival, we must engage our hearts to the occasion. When we engage our heart, we interlock, join, fasten, and set it for and toward the revival (see Jeremiah 30:21-24). When a heart is prepared, the heart will receive great results. Yes, the heart can be set. A set heart, through faith, excels over a Code Blue situation. 1 Chronicles 22:19 says, "Now set your heart and your soul to seek the Lord your God; arise therefore, and build ye the sanctuary of the Lord God, to bring the ark of the covenant of the Lord, and the holy vessels of God, into the house that is to be built to the name of the Lord." (See Proverbs 22:17; Exodus 7:23; and Deuteronomy 32:46 for further study.)

Once the heart is set, engaged, applied, and prepared, there is one more step to consider. We must incline our hearts toward God and the revival; otherwise, we may not make it to the revival services more than one time. Why? A heart that's not inclined for revival will be unconscious to the revival. Heart inclination to the revival will encourage us to open our heart's doors to receive from the Lord that which is necessary. A true, God-ordained revival will allow God to manifest himself. He is there to operate on every heart that is present and open. Revelation 3:20 says, "Behold, I stand at the door, and knock: if any man hear my voice, and open the door, I will come in to him, and will sup with him, and he with me."

Once the heart is inclined, it will motivate the soul, mind, and even the will to be deeply involved with the revival. The will within us must also be set if we are to excel and be successful. By setting the heart first, a set mind and a set will can be established. These three-fold cords cannot be broken: a set mind, a set heart, and a set will.

I must warn those in leadership who plan, construct, and institute revivals that they must keep the hearts of the people in focus and carefully design a revival in which hearts are strengthened, cleaned, encouraged, and drawn closer to God. This way, none will be lost, fail, or cease to function. When there is a revival in progress, you the believer also have the responsibility to apply your heart that you may be heart-informed and gain knowledge. Without heart application there cannot be a true spiritual revival. We must all follow the example set by King Solomon in Ecclesiastes 7:25, who said, "I applied mine heart to know, and to search, and to seek out wisdom, and the reason of things, and to know the wickedness of folly, even of foolishness and madness." (See also Proverbs 2:2 and 2:12; Psalm 90:12; and Ecclesiastes 8:9-16.)

9

MEETING GOD'S HEART REQUIREMENTS

Deuteronomy 10:12: *"And now, Israel, what doth the Lord thy God require of thee, but to fear the Lord thy God, to walk in all his ways, and to love him, and to serve the Lord thy God with all thy heart and with all thy soul."*

In order for this world system to function as it does, there are certain rules, regulations, and requirements that have been set forth that we pay little attention to as we go about our daily lives. Traffic regulations are effective to ensure our safety as we travel on the highways. Business offices have established regulations to make certain the office provides the best service to the consumer. We are faced with daily, weekly, and monthly rules and regulations that are in place for various reasons. Likewise, God also has established requirements that we must meet. Have you seriously considered God's requirements? If we desire to be upright and perfect before God, we must be willing to do what His word says. Only then can we walk in His presence in truth and holiness.

THE PERFECT HEART

Far too many people are operating from a malfunctioning heart. However, God's eyes are roaming to and fro, looking over the whole world like a great magnifying glass, examining the hearts of mankind seeking pure, clean, and perfect hearts (2 Chronicles 16:9).

Let me say this to those who may not believe in heart perfection: God doesn't waste His time looking for something that doesn't exist. God's expectation and requirement is that His people turn away from sin. The Word of God clearly defines what God requires of the believer. God will never ask of us what He hasn't already given us or what He is not willing to make available to us. In Matthew 5:48 we are instructed: "Be ye therefore perfect, even as your Father which is in heaven is perfect." Bible teachers, theologians, scholars, and sincere Bible believers have overlooked this verse for far too long. How can this perfection be obtained? Logically, rationally, and naturally, it would seem that perfection in this life is impossible. How can we possibly be perfect in these vile, sinful bodies, which are bombarded by everything that is unholy, sensual, and sinful? After all, we live next door to satan's children, and we go to school and work alongside wicked children of darkness. Yet, God's Word clearly states that, in spite of our general and individual situations, His requirement is still perfection.

Perfection of the heart is a serious matter. In the Old Testament, Noah and Hezekiah were both described as having perfect hearts (Genesis 6:9, 17:1, and 2 Kings 20:3). If it was required that people walk before God with a perfect heart in Old Testament times prior to the indwelling of the Holy Ghost, how much more important is this requirement today? While a perfect heart is not required by religious denominations, God still requires it. He doesn't allow imperfection where He dwells. God begins to expect perfection as soon as a person is saved. Like a young tree that bursts up through the ground so innocent, pure, and vulnerable to life's surrounding winds and storms, so is a new born again believer. Yet, this young tree is perfect in its youth although its not yet all that it is going to be. It's small, weak and not very pleasurable to look upon; however, its roots are very deep, ensuring continued growth and maturity. It has no leaves, no branches, no notability, but in time, it will grow to be a wonder of the land, rising up to an awesome stature. Birds will build their nests in its branches and abide in its protection. A person passing by will stop on a hot, sunny day to rest under the cool shadows of its branches. Similarly, young Christians grow before and unto the Lord. We grow in love, faith, wisdom, truth, and understanding when our roots are deeply grounded in God's word.

The key is to be perfect in God's sight, even though man may not see you as being perfect. Why? Because perfection is of the spirit and heart, not of the flesh. Who then is righteous and where does righteousness and holiness dwell in us? Remember, man looks on the outward appearance, but God looks on the heart. Greater knowledge, greater understanding, and greater wisdom are necessary to better understand heart perfection. They help guide us and mold us into spiritual perfection in God's sight. Isn't it great to know that God doesn't see us as we see ourselves, but views us through the covering of the shed blood of His son Jesus Christ? Church membership, great titles, and gifts of the spirit are all well and good, but, above all, we must strive for perfection of the heart. God refuses to dwell in an unclean temple. We must dwell in Christ (John 4:12-16), and He dwells in us (2 Corinthians 6:16; Romans 8:9-11). We are then recreated clean and pure vessels, with perfect hearts in His sight. The revelation of perfection is this: nothing God gives us is imperfect. Whatever we have of Him and from Him is perfect. Imperfection and perfection cannot dwell together in our heart or in heaven.

I can remember the time that I purchased my very first car. It was a 2-door, 1949 Chevy, and I paid $325.00 for it. At the time, that was a lot of money for me. I loved that car at first sight. I was 17 years old and thought I was fully grown. Surely I knew more about cars than my father, who was telling me to get the car checked out before I agreed to buy it. I didn't listen to him. It was so pretty on the outside that I paid the dealer with cash on the spot. Something that looked so clean on the outside surely had to be perfect within. How wrong I was and how right my father was. A few days later, I tried to take it through inspection to be approved for tags and insurance, but it was rejected. The car needed more than $600.00 worth of repairs to meet the inspection requirements, codes, and state guidelines. Angrily, I drove back to the dealer who sold me "that piece of junk" only to see him point his finger at the small print on the sales contract saying that "all sales are final and money is nonrefundable." Are we making the same mistakes looking on the outward appearance and not the inward condition of the heart? I believe so.

A New Heart

Ezekiel 36:26-27: "A new heart also will I give you, and a new spirit will I put within you: and I will take away the stony heart out of your flesh, and I will give you an heart of flesh. And I will put my spirit within you, and cause you to walk in my statutes, and ye shall keep my judgments, and do them." (See also Ezekiel 18:2.)

Many say they have a new walk and a new talk, but very few boast of a new heart. No one can have anything new in Christ unless the Lord first deals with his heart. The more we call on God's name, the closer He looks at the heart. In fact, He peers continually into the darkness of man's heart, always looking, listening, and searching for just one soul who will call on His name. Is He ever disappointed? I believe so. We cannot be new creatures without a new heart. When He finds that one soul willing to call on His name, the Lord reaches His nail-scarred hands into that person's heart and draws him to Himself. That believer who is now in the light must totally give his whole heart to Jesus Christ. God is disappointed, even grieved, when He's not allowed to fashion, mold, and establish within that new Christian the type of heart required for a victorious life in Jesus Christ. He is also grieved when anyone dies and their heart is not right. If in the flesh it takes a certain kind of heart to be a president, a prostitute, a cab driver, or a bank manager, what kind of heart is required in the spirit to be a pastor, teacher, evangelist, or servant of God? A new heart is mandatory for the new life, new relationship, and new destiny.

We must meet God's heart requirement if we are to be heart-approved. We'll be approved if our new minds are set, our souls anchored, and our new hearts fully prepared.

Negative Heart Habits Must Be Broken

Webster's dictionary defines "habits" as a pattern of action that is acquired (learned behavior); something that has become so automatic that it is difficult to break. Because the heart is directly connected to the mind, the will, our emotions, and our soul, negative habits have a detrimental effect upon the heart. Habits are performed so unconsciously that we often don't think about what our hands are doing, what our mouths are saying, what our ears are hearing, what our eyes are watching, or what our emotions are feeling. But habits—good or bad—have the power to manipulate the heart. However, it is not impossible to break our old habits. Negative heart habits are a serious matter and must be broken, especially since Christ dwells within our hearts and the issues of life flow from the heart.

SIN—THE ROOT OF ALL NEGATIVE HEART HABITS

The greatest devastation visited upon mankind is the plague of sin. Unlike the flood in the days of Noah, which receded after a period of time, sin has never receded; instead, it has gotten progressively worse with each generation. Death, sickness, and disease are co-joined within the plague of sin, but most important of all, separation from God and spiritual death are the final judgment of unconfessed sin. Habitual sin is and has always been a key issue between God and man. Mankind was not created by God to live a life of sin. Billions of dollars are spent in an effort to correct the problems stemming from the hearts that are steeped in sin. When will America wise up and allow the gospel message to be front page news in the newspapers? What if our court systems started sentencing habitual offenders to 20 years of Bible study and church service as a means of rehabilitation? Perhaps then many of society's problems would be remedied.

Sin is an aggressive, offensive spirit against God. God gave us His laws and commandments as a defensive measure to counter habitual sins. From the age of about two years old, our sin nature begins to manifest; selfishness, anger, and rebelliousness war against unselfishness, kindness, and obedience. Thus, the wars of the human heart begin and negative habits are made. The sins we committed when we were sinners are habits that have to be broken by the Holy Spirit and the Word of God.

Good and bad habits fashion our lifestyle. Bad negative habits keep our hearts from being perfect and pure. Many times negative heart habits are developed from doing things that are seemingly innocent on the surface, such as girl watching or boy watching. However, underlying the enjoyment of watching "beautiful" people, a spirit of lust may creep in unawares. All of a sudden an appetite for pornography develops, or instead of just watching, one begins to daydream and fantasize about the beautiful people he or she was "just watching." Now, don't get me wrong, nothing is wrong with looking, but when it goes beyond looking–WATCH OUT! A Code Red warning signal is flashing!

The heart is directly connected to the mind, will, emotions, and soul; therefore, when a negative habit becomes rooted in the heart, the heart regulates the habit, and the habit then regulates our lives. Take for instance the mere act of talking to someone about a vexing situation regarding a fellow believer. We may say we are only telling this thing so that others may pray about it, but our heart knows the truth. The heart will allow us to believe that we are telling something for the good of a sister or brother, but it knows that what we are really doing is gossiping, slandering, or telling lies. Lying to ourselves about our motives and intents is a Code Red habit of the heart.

BREAKING NEGATIVE HEART HABITS

God must become our habitual pattern, otherwise we may fall out of His will, be divided within, become confused, and be subject to be hurt. The easiest way to break a bad habit is to simply stop. We must determine to focus our hearts in a new direction, saturate our minds with the Word, and habitually submit our will to God. We read God's Word with our eyes; it then enters the mind, travels to our heart, and touches our soul. Reading God's Word on a daily basis is a great habit that protects us all from serious matters of the heart (Psalm 119:11). God's Word prepares the heart for forming positive habits.

It is extremely important to prepare our hearts for God. 2 Chronicles 12:14 says, "And he did evil, because he prepared not his heart to seek the Lord," and 2 Chronicles 20:33 says, "Howbeit the high places were not taken away: for as yet the people had not prepared their hearts unto the God of their fathers." One way to do this is to be aware of God's plan for our lives.

When will the Church realize that the sins of the heart hinder us from being heaven-ready, God prepared, and heart-approved. We must meet God's qualifications and expectations in order to reach our expected end.

Jeremiah 29:11 says, "For I know the thoughts that I think toward you, saith the Lord, thoughts of peace, and not of evil, to give you an expected end." This means that God has a specific plan for each of us. God's expectations for His creation never included sin and death. Yet, due to the sin nature, sin and death are lodged in the genes and spiritual arteries of our heart from birth, changing our destiny and our fellowship with the Lord. For our divine protection, we must meet God's heart requirements.

Knowing God's will, plan, and purposes for our lives is of utmost importance. God has imparted to all mankind defenses against our inherited sin nature. We must fashion our lifestyle in accordance with the Word of God and walk daily in the ways of God with all of our heart and soul. We must cease trying to fashion God into our image and remember that we were created in His image. Due to Code Blue, many of us need to be recreated again saying "Create in me, Lord, a pure and clean heart."

SECRET HEART SINS

Many give birth to a sin never realizing that it has been "gestating" within them. Few of us truly know exactly what God's grace and mercy are covering in our lives. We go through tests, trials, and seasons of troubles, which are allowed by God so that these secret sins may be revealed. When they arise, don't panic and don't try to hide them or suppress them—get rid of them!

LEAKY HEARTS

Negative heart habits, thoughts, and imaginations that are allowed to remain within us will cause the positive things sown in the heart to leak out. If your heart is leaky, you will find that the spiritual activities you once gained strength and joy from are no longer appealing. Time spent in prayer and communion with God becomes dull and boring; time spent in reading and studying God's Word is no longer satisfying to your spirit; and even time spent enjoying fellowship with other believers is no longer enjoyable. What happened to cause this? Negative heart habits have consumed the spirit man, causing spiritual vitamins to seep out. A heart that is not wholly given to God has no protection. We must realize that whatever we feed the most will be the strongest. A leaky heart makes us weak, unstable Christians.

FILLED TO MEET HIS APPROVAL

The God we serve is a heart filler. He fills us with all of His goodness, giving us His spirit and nature that we may fulfill His Word and His requirements. He fills us with His righteousness (Matthew 5:6), the Holy Ghost (Luke 1:15-67, Acts 2:4, Acts 4:8-31, and 9:17), and wisdom (Luke 2:40). The Lord also fills the heart with truth, love, joy, wisdom, peace, His word, grace, and salvation to meet His requirements and purpose. We fall short of God's requirements when we mix the things of this world with the things of God. Worldly cares, like fiery darts, pierce the pure and clean heart. They cut and rip the wise and perfect heart until the Holy Spirit becomes grieved and the lifestyle of that person is rejected. It is true that we must guard, keep and protect our heart at all times for out of it flow the issues of life (Proverbs 4:23). The Bible is full of instructions for us on how to gain knowledge that will enable us to meet God's requirements.

What God requires of us is far less than what He has promised us and what He has done for us. However, pride (self-worth) and the "I, me, my, and mine (selfishness) syndrome" have consumed many hearts, causing many souls to perish. We have power to think in our heart; therefore, if our mind and thoughts are stayed on Jesus, we can direct and set our hearts in the right direction to be God-approved.

EXAMINE YOURSELF

Meeting God's requirements can only occur if we thoroughly examine our hearts. In 1 Corinthians 11:28 we read, "But let a man examine himself, and so let him eat of that bread, and drink of that cup." We must also ask the Lord to examine us. Psalm 26:2 adds, "Examine me, O Lord, and prove me; try my reins and my heart."

The term *examine*, according to Webster's Dictionary, means "to inspect with care; to analyze, test, investigate, scan, study, explore, sift, audit, consider and take an inventory of." The term *judge* may be used in the same context. We are instructed to judge ourselves. We don't judge to condemn but rather to know what is right or wrong within us. Self-examination isn't popular in the Christian lifestyle, but it must be done. One day we will all stand before the judgment seat of God to give account. Woe be to the one who doesn't meet God's heart requirements simply because he didn't take the time to examine himself! In Hosea 4:1-6, God talks about His people being destroyed for lack of knowledge. I believe He made a reference to the knowledge of His Word, will, purpose, and heart. I would like to introduce to the Body of Christ the word *kardiognostes*, the study, learning, and knowledge of the heart. We must examine our hearts to know what is there. (See Acts 1:24; 15:8.)

I am the kind of person that detests going to the doctor. I simply hate the examination the doctor puts me through. And yet, I know that if I don't undergo a doctor's exam regularly, I could become sick, even to the point of death, with a disease that could have been prevented.

The point here is that most Christians go through the same ordeal on a continual basis, avoiding self-examination until something goes wrong. Neglecting to perform a daily self-examination places our heart at risk of becoming tainted, torn, wounded, diseased or sick without our knowledge. Because of Christians' neglect to examine themselves, the Body of Christ is seriously ill. Faith is on trial, there's no godly joy and peace, the Word of God is seldom manifested in our lives, and the truth is

133

rarely recognized. The best cure of all is prevention. A sick spirit, soul, and body cannot meet the requirements of God. Our heart and body speak to us and we need to hear them. No doctor knows more about us than our Creator, and few ever go to a doctor unless they "feel" that something is wrong. When they go into the doctor's office, the first thing that the doctor asks is "What is wrong with you?" God has not yet allowed the medical profession to develop a device that will show forth the condition of our spiritual heart. Therefore, let each of us examine his own heart, judging all things that emulate from and in the mind, soul, desires, and emotions. Let us daily judge our many thoughts and imaginations, our love life, our prayer life, time spent in the Word and worship, and even how we feel about the smallest things of God. We can't afford to take anything for granted. Many serious Code Red and Code Blue spiritual matters begin in the heart and can be prevented if detected early through self-examination.

God is who He is and can't help but to do what He does. He examines all things and every heart. He tests the heart, knows the heart, fixes the heart and in the end, approves or disapproves the heart. But He doesn't do so arbitrarily. He tells us how to obtain His approval.

All of the instructions bestowed upon us, which come from the Lord, are for our benefit. If we are obedient to the guidelines found in God's Word, we will be in perfect harmony and union with God. Not only has God provided us with all that is necessary for heart perfection, He has given us the most important benefit of all–the Spirit of His beloved Son to dwell within us. The Holy Spirit will teach us all things if we allow Him to. The indwelling presence of the Holy Spirit gives us access to holy perfection through our continual obedience, prayer, faith, and repentance. Prayer keeps us in harmony with God; faith keeps us in God; and we are then seen in the spirit realm as perfect.

However, a problem that I see as I daily strive to walk before the Lord with a perfect heart is that I may not know exactly what state my heart is in. I may think and believe I'm okay; I may even feel like I am okay. But I often remember that God does not think, feel and believe like I do; therefore, I must remain before

Him in humble submission so that I may be transformed into His image. I must continually seek to attain that higher level of perfection that can only be found in and through Christ Jesus. I die daily to the world, flesh, and all evil and press forward to the higher calling in Christ. Again, self-examination is key.

Have you had your spiritual heart check-up today? Has your spiritual heart been tested? Will it pass the eternal life exam? Evaluate your own heart's position by taking note of your daily thoughts, imaginations, desires, and plans. Are they pure and holy? This walk of faith is also a *see, say,* and *do* journey. *Say* what the Word says, *do* what the Word says do, and *see* that God's way is better. We must *stop, look,* and *listen*–stop what we're doing wrong, look at the cost if we continue, and listen to what God is saying and what He has said in His Word. Don't take a chance with your heart; the price is too high if you miss the mark. Examine yourself on a daily basis and stay before God. Seek to be purified and heart-approved. Worship God and pray without ceasing.

THE BLOOD

Without the shedding of blood, it would be impossible for any of our hearts to appear perfect before God. Leviticus 5:9 says, "And he shall sprinkle of the blood of the sin offering upon the side of the altar; and the rest of the blood shall be wrung out at the bottom of the altar; it is a sin offering." The blood of the Lamb (Christ) protects our spiritual heart. His blood continually washes, cleanses, and removes sinful contamination that would render our hearts imperfect. Once we've reached heart perfection, God seals the heart. We have been blood-washed, blood-bought and covered with love. Our hearts will reach perfection only when we place them in God's hands and allow them to be cleansed by the blood of Christ.

A PERFECT AND LOVING HEART

You may be familiar with the lyrics of a popular song, which say, "What the world needs now is love." Love, however, is only a part of the answer to the world's conditions. The whole truth is that what the world needs now is a perfect and loving heart. Love is a major component to attaining heart perfection. Without God's love, the heart cannot be perfect and it cannot reach the level of character necessary for heart perfection. Love can break up and destroy the strongholds of satan and put to death the fleshly desires that are prone to arise in us. The perfect love of God, however, cannot be seeded in a contaminated and imperfect heart. Every man born of a woman is born with a spiritual, congenital heart disorder. But there is hope for us. In essence, Christ became our heart donor, our heart fixer, and our heart regulator, when He gave His life for us on the Cross. He was wounded in His heart that we might be healed in ours.

MOVE ON INTO PERFECTION

Perfection requires that we totally surrender to God and remain committed to walking in righteousness before Him. It's a walk in which we will be tempted to rebel daily. Our Creator alone is able to create a perfect heart in us. King David knew this and asked God to perform this great task (Psalm 51:10). God is the potter; we are the clay. It's so simple, but many believers have missed it. Our hearts must be God-filled, God-controlled, and God-covered. Heart perfection requires us to allow the Holy Spirit to anchor our souls and bring our flesh under subjection to the will, ways, and works of God. This is how we move into perfection (Hebrews 6:1). It is imperative that we surrender control of our lives to Jesus Christ. The flesh will always war against the heart, but the heart can have victory if it is surrendered to God.

HEART ANCHORED

The Holy Spirit is there to anchor our hearts and souls and render them clean and perfect in the sight of God. Pray that your anchor holds. God will not keep your heart clean and pure if you don't want it to be kept. You can backslide before complete perfection takes place. Be not deceived though, for God is not mocked. Whatsoever is sown in the heart shall also be reaped from the heart. Therefore, sow the Word, sow love, sow joy, and sow peace so that the soul and heart can be changed into righteousness.

10

WITH ALL MY HEART

Proverbs 3:5: *"Trust in the Lord with all thine heart; and lean not unto thine own understanding."*

God does not want half of our heart. No, He wants us to give Him our whole heart. To give means to impart, to present, to dispense, to deliver, to remit, or to relinquish. We must be willing to give our old dirty hearts to God in order to receive our new and improved hearts specifically designed for us. When we give the Lord our whole heart, it's the greatest move against satan in guaranteeing our victory over the attacks of Code Red and Code Blue Sin. We are in essence giving God access to our whole self—who we are, what we think, and what we do. We are saying, "I'm yours, Lord. Try me now and see if I can be completely yours."

When we give all of our heart to God, it means we are giving Him all He desires, requires, and demands. Some people give God all their tithes and offerings and all their time to their church, family and friends but then hold back when it's time to give all of their heart to God. Whether this withholding is done out of fear or ignorance is unimportant. It is for the requirement of God for us to surrender our whole hearts. Because of our failure to do this, the distance between God's heart and the heart of the church has grown exponentially. Mark 7:6-7 says, "He answered and said unto them, Well hath Esaias prophesied of you hypocrites, as it is written, This people honoureth me with their lips, but their heart is far from me. Howbeit in vain do they worship me, teaching for doctrines the commandments men." If our hearts are far from God, nothing else we do matters.

Today, God is speaking loudly to the Body of Christ from a passage of scripture found in Mark 12:28-31. I've taken the liberty to term this passage "The Gospel of All." The Gospel of All speaks to how we do what we do and it is very clear regarding what God expects from us. It says "And one of the scribes came, and having heard them reasoning together, and perceiving that he had answered them well, asked him, Which is the first commandment of all? And Jesus answered him, The first of all the commandments is, Hear, O Israel; The Lord our God is one Lord: And thou shalt love the Lord thy God with all thy heart, and with all thy soul, and with all thy mind, and with all thy strength: this is the first commandment. And the second is like, namely this, Thou shalt love thy neighbour as thyself. There is none other commandment greater than these." God wants nothing less than it all—all our heart, all our soul, and all our mind, and all our strength. Why? He is Lord of all, the God of all living. All powerful, knowing, loving, and all heart.

Once God has our hearts, He will never let go. That's one of the reasons that satan so desperately tries to hide the serious heart message of God from the body of Christ. The teaching of how to give your heart wholly to Jesus Christ is no longer a viable part of today's ministry; instead, we concentrate on outward things such as money, clothes, health, houses, and land. But today, God is flipping the script and turning the page saying, "My child, give me your heart." A given life must accompany a given heart. Although there are many covenants contained in the Bible, there is one that requires a closer inspection. It's the covenant between your heart and God's heart, and is described in Ezekiel 36:26-28, which states, "A new heart also will I give you, and a new spirit will I put within you: and I will take away the stony heart out of your flesh, and I will give you an heart of flesh. And I will put my spirit within you, and cause you to walk in my statutes, and ye shall keep my judgments, and do them. And ye shall dwell in the land that I gave to your fathers; and ye shall be my people, and I will be your God."

What is the problem and why do we hold back in giving God what He really wants? Of what are we fearful? Beloved, God is worthy to receive the most precious gift that we have. He has never asked of His children what He has not given himself. The Bible declares that He loved the world so much, that He gave His only begotten Son (John 3:16). Before Jesus was manifested on the earth, He dwelt in the heart of God. God is now saying, "Do what I did and give me your most beloved possession—your heart." The only place the Lord desires to dwell within the earth is in the heart.

SEEK HIM WITH YOUR WHOLE HEART

In addition to giving God our whole heart, we must also diligently seek and search for Him with all of our heart. This is accomplished through searching the Scriptures daily and seeking Him through worship prayer, fasting, and supplication. The foolishness of man is demonstrated when he is lifted up in his own conceit, going his own way and doing his own thing. Many people don't give God a second thought throughout the day. However, God can take the most ordinary thing to speak to our hearts. We must remain ready to find the Lord, for if we diligently seek Him, we shall find Him. Look for Him in the words of your spouse, children, co-workers, and friends. Look for Him in the way the flower blooms, the rain falls, and the sun shines. God can give you a message as you glance through the newspaper or as you watch television. When you are in a seeking mode, God will take every opportunity to make sure you find Him.

THE GOD OF RELEASE

Proverbs 23:26: *"My son, give me thine heart, and let thine eyes observe my ways."* Ezekiel 11:19: *"And I will give them one heart, and I will put a new spirit within you; and I will take the stony heart out of their flesh, and will give them an heart of flesh."*

When we give God our hearts, God, who is a God of release and restoration, will abide there and begin to reconstruct, rebuild, and restore the damage that has been done to our hearts through a sinful life. He is waiting to release you from the pain and memory of abuse hidden in the deep recesses of your heart. He wants to heal you from the brokenness of failed marriages and unhealthy relationships. His hands are outstretched and His arms are opened wide waiting for you to come to Him, heavy and laden with the burden of life's hurts, pains, and defeat. He's waiting for you to give Him your life and all of your heart.

THE GOD OF LOVE

When you give God your heart to dwell in, He who is love will first whitewash your heart with His love, then equip your heart to show forth His love. The light that cannot be hidden shines forth from a heart filled with the love of God. When God's love dwells in the heart, man's hatefulness will not have the power to damage it again. His love is a shield from the fiery darts of Code Red and Code Blue arrows. His love is the sealant of the heart.

Beloved, God is saying today, "My people don't know, they don't consider or count the cost. They don't consider My ways, My knowledge, My will, or My thoughts. They forget me until a crisis or a need arises, but I'm a God of the heart, and I answer all according to My will and the condition or position of the heart. Hear, My people and consider this." I encourage you to heed the words of 1 Samuel 12:24: "Only fear the Lord, and serve him in truth with all your heart: for consider how great things he hath done for you."

A CHANGE OF HEART

The heart is a spiritual system that works to release all that abides within it. It makes plans, holds knowledge and memory, and communes with the mind, soul, and will. Therefore, when the heart is not totally given to God and broken to His will, it becomes the most dangerous weapon upon the earth. We are governed by what our heart contains and there can be no change of life or lifestyle until there is a change of heart.

According to Webster's Dictionary the term *change* means "an alteration, a reconstruction, a transformation, and a redirection." Christ continually knocks on the door of every heart that He might impart a change (Revelation 3:20). If we open the door, He will come into our heart, cleanse and wash it, and set up His base of operations. One day the Lord said to me, *"Don, your heart is not right with me."* Immediately I saw in a vision something that looked good to eat on the outside but was decayed, vile and withered within. It made me sick to look at the vision, but I knew this was my very own heart that the Lord was showing me. I immediately repented. I began to ask the Lord to take all of my heart, cleanse it, make it fit for His use. He then let me know that a change of heart must take place. Today I can truly say that I have been changed, but He is still working on my heart. Maybe I am not yet what I should be, but praise His name that I am not what I used to be. We all must come to the understanding that there is a need for change, especially when something within us does not line up with the Word within our spirit.

I will never forget the day my wife and I went to purchase a house that was just lovely to look at—on the outside. The exterior was just beautiful. Oh, how we wanted that house, until we went inside and saw its shattered walls, broken utilities, and filthy condition. We refused to purchase the house because the inside needed too many repairs. It was not fit for our use. Thankfully, God never deems our hearts to be too much work for Him to purchase. He is willing to make the repairs that are necessary for our hearts to be fit for His use. The cost is not the issue His purpose is. Unlike mankind God never sees cost as being more important than His purpose. God has made the way for all of us to be changed within; Jesus Christ is the only way. He must dwell within us, and we must remain in Him. That is why the Lord said, "I am the way, the truth, and the life" (John 14:6). A spiritual heart transplant, a gospel heart bypass, and a brand new heart change comes only by the work of the Holy Spirit in our hearts. He works as we work. There is not one unsaved person on the face of this earth who can inherit salvation eternally without a heart change or a major spiritual heart operation.

Have you given Him all of your heart? Are you sure? Without our hearts being totally released unto God, our eternal destiny is held in question and the many hours we spend in a church, in prayer, in reading God's Word, and even communicating with our Heavenly Father may all be in vain. Let us remember that if satan can talk to God and be heard of God, how much more will God hear us when we come and talk to Him. All God wants to do is save us from the greatest enemy of man—his own heart. Don't take your spiritual walk for granted. Have a heart checkup today. Talk to the Great Heart Physician, and He will reveal to you the knowledge that you seek of Him.

11

THE LOST HEART

Luke 19:10: *"For the Son of man is come to seek and to save that which was lost."*

It is commonly believed that the Bible is the most bought and least read of all books in the world. The Bible originated from the heart of God and was specifically designed and intended to dwell in the heart of man. The Word of God is God's power source for our heart's actions toward Him. Christ, the Word of God, came from God's heart to dwell in our hearts, redeeming and reconnecting us back to God. Very few believers have seen Christ's heart even though it's available to every race, creed, and nationality. The Bible is the only book of salvation, yet someone once said that "If there's any book in my house covered with dust, it's my Bible!" The Bible is good news from God's heart. If it is obeyed, the power and truth found in God's revealed word can save and keep us from sin and eternal damnation. It may be spelled out like this: B-etter I-nvestigate B-efore L-eaving E-arth. Through reading the Bible, a person can learn about the difference between a lost heart and a saved heart.

A lost heart is a heart that is no longer visible or available to God. It is a heart that is not found and has gone astray. It is not being used to do good, nor does it have a godly purpose. A heart that is spiritually ruined, destroyed, arrogant, distracted, and distraught is lost. A lost heart is insensitive to God's plan of salvation, it is without the benefits of the Cross, and it exists without repentance. It may also be listless, spiritually lifeless, incomplete, lonely, dreadful, and potentially deadly. A lost heart is dark, without hope or light—an enemy of God.

In contrast, a saved heart is a heart that has been delivered from danger, rescued from eternal suffering, and excused from the penalty of death. A saved heart is a believing heart that is preserved in Christ and that has been granted eternal salvation. It has been made free from the power and bondage of sin. A saved heart has been brought safely through, having escaped the world system through grace by faith in Christ Jesus. It has thus obtained favor with God and has become an enemy of satan. A saved heart is one that has been washed in Christ's blood and baptized with repentance. It has been redeemed and reconstructed by the indwelling of the Holy Spirit.

Lost hearts are lost because of sin. Lost hearts miss the mark and come short of God's mark for man. Lost hearts commit transgression of divine law and violate God's moral principles because they are steeped in sin. Sin is the source of wrong actions and of an inward element producing outward acts against God, and it is a governing principle of power that flows within and manifests itself outwardly. It operates in various ways identified in scripture as iniquity (immorality), Enmity (hatred), lawlessness, and transgressions.

A lost heart is polluted, deceived, defiled, unsaved, and dangerous. It may dwell secretly within a preacher, pastor, teacher, evangelist, deacon, minister, usher, or missionary. The serious matter of a lost heart is that it lives daily in a Code Blue state of peril. Every lost soul is dead in their sins while they yet live. 1 Corinthians 15:56-57 says, "The sting of death is sin; and the strength of sin is the law. But thanks be to God, which giveth us the victory through our Lord Jesus Christ." (For further study, see Ephesians 2:1-10.)

A lost, sinful heart always operates in a Code Red State under the authority of Code Blue. It's only by true repentance and through receiving the Lord Jesus Christ as Lord and Savior that the lost heart is made free. Our heart is the doorway between heaven and hell, and its state of holiness or unholiness determines our eternal destination. When sin controls the heart, it takes the heart hostage, controlling the mind and actions and perverting the believer's testimony of the saving grace of God (Matthew 15:7-9; 2 Corinthians 4:3).

The lost heart reigns over today's society. It is more deadly than the largest earthquake or the biggest flood and fiercer than the widest forest fire or hurricane. It's more deadly than the coral or cobra snake and kills more each year than the atomic bomb could. When the lost heart is allowed to flourish, it ruins the soul, stifles the mind, confuses the emotions, and makes the flesh vulnerable to devils and demons. Just as the saved heart has the power to operate three or four good works at the same time, such as preaching, witnessing, and teaching, the lost heart can also operate three or four evil works at the same time, such as raping, murdering, and lying. The saved heart is controlled and guided by God, but the unsaved heart gets its orders from satan.

How can those on the road to eternal condemnation and judgment recover and be saved? The answer is found in Revelation 3:20 which says, "Behold, I stand at the door and knock: if any man hear my voice, and open the door, I will come in to him, and will sup with him, and he with me." Even though Christ knocks on every heart's door saying "Let me in, salvation and deliverance has come to your house," the lost heart bolts the door, throws away the key, and says "Oh no, not me, I'm not ready yet!" The heart then grows harder each time it rejects God and goes deeper into the darkness and degradation of Code Red Sin.

A REPENTANT HEART

Acts 2:38-39: "Then Peter said to them, Repent, and be baptized every one of you in the name of Jesus Christ for the remission of sins, and ye shall receive the gift of the Holy Ghost. For the promise is unto you, and to your children, and to all that are afar off, even as many as the Lord our God shall call." (See also 2 Peter 3:9). There is hope for the lost heart if it will repent. According to Webster's Dictionary, *repent* means "to feel regret and become sorry for past conduct; to have a change of mind." The key is to know that this process must first begin within the heart. The mind cannot produce true repentance on its own. Change must first begin from within the heart.

After many seasons of ups and downs, attacks of the enemy, doubt and unbelief, trials and tribulations, and sins, the repentant heart declares "It is finished! Lying, stealing, and cheating are finished! Fornication, homosexuality, and adultery are finished!" The sinner no longer wants sin to rule their heart, life, mind, and soul. True heart repentance renders the heart pure and clean, worthy to be filled with and sealed by the Holy Spirit of God.

Heart salvation is an ongoing process. God continually works on the heart, preparing it for eternal life. Salvation denotes deliverance and preservation. The term *salvation* is used in Hebrews 11:7 to describe the spiritual and eternal deliverance granted immediately by God to those who accept His conditions of repentance. It can only be obtained through faith in the Lord Jesus (Act 4:12); and upon confession of Him as Lord (Romans 10:10). For this purpose, the gospel is the saving instrument (Romans 1:16; Ephesians 1:13) that God uses to deliver us from the bondage of sin. Sin always promises what it cannot deliver, but God always delivers on His promises.

In simple terms, to be saved means to be free from the penalty, the price, and the judgment of eternal condemnation. The minute we give our hearts to God's salvation principles, God begins working on the heart to prepare it for eternal marriage to Him. God performs this through the outpouring of His Holy Spirit into our hearts once repentance is complete. There is an inner you (the spiritual man) and an outer you (the fleshly man). The inner you is the eternal you. If the inner you is void of the knowledge of God, he's Code Blue dead while he yet lives. How do I know? I lived a sinner's life for over 28 years.

"GOOD" BUT LOST

I've known many unsaved people who are taught good morals and manners from their youth. As adults, they live what they consider to be morally clean lives. Some feel that they're as "good" as any Christian because of the things they don't do.

Their lost hearts have deceived them though, because, morally good or not, they are still sinners bound for hell.

God writes the name of the person with a saved heart in the Lamb's Book of Life. I pray that all of who that still have a lost heart will realize that the Lord paid for every one of your sins and that the world and satan have done nothing for you. Satan deceives and gathers souls to himself by using enticement, binding, luring, and deception. We have the power to receive the salvation of God into our hearts or to reject it. My friends, it's your heart that determines all things on your behalf! It's heart action resulting from true heart repentance that God responds to. Therefore, it is the Lord alone who saves the heart, and it is His work within us that anchors the soul. It's not what you believe but *in whom* you believe that determines the state of your heart. For example, most people believe that Jesus was the Son of God, that He died on the Cross, that he was buried and rose on the third day and that the Bible is the Word of God. But that's not enough, for if they haven't totally given their hearts to Him and received Him, they are still lost. For years church leadership has "opened the doors to the church" that the lost may be saved. This doesn't work. God wants sinners to open the doors to their hearts and let Him come in. Neither has the "altar call" pleased the Lord, for it is a "heart call" that is required.

The heart must be contrite, and the spirit must be broken to God's will in order for the heart to be filled with God's Word. A heart transplant or some type of inner operation must also take place. It's an arduous, painful process as God cleanses, changes, and renews your heart.

MICROWAVE SALVATION

"Microwave salvation" is becoming more popular than ever in these last days. What I mean by this is that individuals want immediate, quick-fix results without putting in effort and hard work. The preacher calls a person up, tells him or her to say a few words, and presto, he declares that person to be saved. It's the latest fad, but it doesn't get the job done in the heart. Words are not enough; the heart must be surrendered. Christ must be real in our lives and hearts. We must open the Bible, read it, receive it, and confess it for the remainder of our lives. Christ at Calvary made provisions for all sinners to be saved, but not all sinners will be saved. "Microwave salvation" says just believe and you got it; however, heart salvation states you must be born again and made brand new, old things must die and new things must be birthed. 2 Corinthians 5:17 says, "Therefore if any man be in Christ, he is a new creature; old things are passed away; behold, all things are become new." (See also John 3:1-7.)

Believing, trusting, and confessing are important components in maintaining new life in Christ; however keep in mind the fall of satan—he knew God, talked with God and believed in God. However, it was the thoughts and imaginations within his heart that caused his fall. By his evil thoughts, wicked imaginations, and lustful desires he became condemned and contaminated. By his imaginations he became wicked, evil, obscene, debased, polluted in his heart, unclean, unfit, and unworthy. God threw him out of heaven into outer darkness. This clearly reveals that one may "say and believe" that he is saved but not be in his heart. It may well be that the person you think of as the most holy, sanctified and set apart is in fact headed for hell. The lost heart is the most cunning, sly, and deceptive thing on earth, and it can fool anyone except for Christ. Although you may not know the heart of another, you can know your own heart and Christ's heart. If you know your heart is lost, I hope you will turn to God for salvation today.

THE BEGINNINGS OF THE LOST HEART

When God created mankind, He created us with clean and perfect hearts. However, through satan's deception of Adam and Eve and their subsequent fall, the human heart became lost and far from perfect. Instead of being called sons of God, man is now referred to as sinners, the unsaved, condemned souls, or workers of iniquity. Many people have asked me, "Why didn't God just destroy satan?" I ask them, "Why didn't God destroy Adam and Eve?" Both had disobeyed God. However, God had already provided a way of escape for man, and it didn't include their destruction. God chose to neutralize rebellion with love. The Lord knew that He himself would have to go to the Cross and die for all mankind. God kept this fact hidden within His own heart, for no man knew in the beginning that the Lamb of God was destined to be slain from the foundation of the world (Revelation 13:8). I believe this means that within God's heart, Christ was slain even before He said "Let there be light."

REMEDIES FOR THE LOST HEART

To preserve mankind, God gave forth the law, and under the law, salvation came as a result of works and obedience. However, the law could not provide man with permanent deliverance from his sins and his unrighteous heart. The prophets knew God, yet they all sinned. David sinned with Bathsheba. Abraham lied about his wife Sarah to Pharaoh. Samson lied and acted in unholy ways. Though the law was good, it didn't keep man from thinking wicked thoughts and evil imaginations, and it did not change the motives and intents of his heart. Therefore, God went beyond the law and commandments and gave promises of a new heart and a new unbreakable covenant. In Ezekiel 36:26, God said, "A new heart also will I give you, and a new spirit will I put within you: and I will take away the stony heart out of your flesh, and I will give you an heart of flesh." (For further study, see Ezekiel 11:19; 18:31.) God is a God of the new. He makes all things new—brand new. He is new every morning (Lamentations 3:23). In Christ we are clothed with new garments, we sing a new song, have a new name, a new life, a new covenant, and a new and living way. We become as fresh bread and fruitful trees. Our brand new heart is fully prepared for the new heaven and new earth. Before salvation, we may have been addicted to money, drugs, sex, and other Code Blue Sins of this world. After salvation, however, we should be addicted to God, love, the Word, worship, prayer, praise, His presence and faith. Instead of becoming intoxicated by alcohol, we are filled with His Spirit, and we drink living water from a fountain that shall never run dry. Because we have a new heart, we also have a new relationship and a new destiny as we take God at His Word.

Romans 10:8-10 outlines the steps we must take in order to receive a new and saved heart in Christ. "But what saith it? The word is nigh thee, even in thy mouth, and in thy heart: that is, the word of faith, which we *preach*; That if thou shalt confess with thy mouth the Lord Jesus, and shalt *believe in thine heart* that God hath raised him from the dead, thou shalt be saved. For with *the heart* man believeth unto righteousness; and with the mouth confession is made unto salvation." This scripture instructs us to preach the Word from our hearts, to confess Jesus as Lord, and to believe (have faith) from our hearts unto righteousness. This process allows us to be born again (John 3:3-6), filled with the Holy Spirit through repentance (Acts 2:38), and adopt a new lifestyle. In Romans 10:17, we also see that faith comes by hearing—our ears are great passageways to the heart, as are our eyes and mouth. Only when we follow the instructions outlined in the passages discussed above can our hearts become vessels that are pleasing to God.

God's ultimate judgment of a lost heart that does not open itself to Him is destruction of them all at judgment day. The lost heart is anti-God in nature and of no value in structure in and of itself. It must be rebirthed, recharged, restored, renewed and reconstructed in order for it to find favor with God. Once a person follows the guidelines of Romans 10:9, the heart will be changed, declared righteous, and brought to a state of standing that is pure and clean. However, confession from the heart in this passage of scripture is a lifestyle, not just a one time utterance! The Holy Spirit, who dwells within us upon salvation, will eventually bring about this kind of lifestyle in us through His daily work in our hearts. Please don't let anyone tell you that you don't need the Holy Spirit to be saved Don't believe them, for it's a lie, and it will keep your heart in the lost posture. It will cause you to view salvation from outward to inward rather than from inward to outward. Salvation is an inward work of God on the heart, will, and mind. On the day of resurrection, God will not look on our bodies; rather, He will look upon us to find His attributes within our heart. His love, Jesus' blood, our faith, and God's Word must be there. God's Son, the Lord Jesus Christ, especially must be within our hearts. The Holy Spirit preserves, protects, and fashions the heart from His dwelling place within man, which renders us ready for God's inspection.

THE HEART OF KING SOLOMON

King Solomon, who was the son of King David and the wisest man who ever lived, had a right heart before God. In 1 Kings 3:9 he asked God what every king, judge, or leader should ask God: "Give therefore thy servant an understanding heart to judge thy people, that I may discern between good and bad: for who is able to judge thy so great a people?" Even for those of us who are not rulers, this request is a wonderful example of a proper request to bring to God. Because Solomon didn't ask God for money, long life, riches, or power, his request touched God's heart. God responded, answering him in 1 Kings 3:12 by saying, "Behold, I have done according to thy words: lo, I have given thee a wise and an understanding heart; so that there was none like thee before thee, neither after thee shall any arise like unto thee."

Solomon's petition was pleasing to God, and it is interesting to note that Solomon followed his father David's advice when forming his prayer. When David realized that Solomon, his son, was his replacement as king, he encouraged Solomon regarding how to excel in God. David knew the destructiveness of a deceived heart, and he counseled Solomon to be perfect and upright in heart before God. In 1 Chronicles 28:9, David says, "And thou Solomon, my son, know thou the God of thy father, and serve him with a perfect heart and with a willing mind: for the Lord searcheth all hearts, and understandeth all the imaginations of the thoughts: if thou seek him, he will be found of thee; but if thou forsake him, he will cast thee off for ever."

Just before his death, David then went to God himself. He stood up before the congregation and prayed, "I know also, my God, that thou triest the heart, and hast pleasure in uprightness.

151

As for me, in the uprightness of mine heart I have willingly offered all these things: and now have I seen with joy thy people, which are present here, to offer willingly unto thee. O Lord God of Abraham, Isaac, and of Israel, our fathers, keep this forever in the imagination of the thoughts of the heart of thy people, and prepare their heart unto thee: And give unto Solomon my son a perfect heart, to keep thy commandments, thy testimonies, and thy statutes, and to do all these things, and to build the palace, for the which I have made provision" (1 Chronicles 29: 17-19). Here we see the importance of a father praying for his son. Many of Solomon's good choices can be attributed to David's godly example. However, Solomon was still ultimately responsible for his own heart.

The Lord answered David's prayer and gave Solomon a perfect heart. However, he didn't take away Solomon's right and will to choose. Unfortunately, Solomon made some wrong choices and didn't keep his heart perfect before God. Solomon loved many strange women, including the daughter of Pharaoh. He took for himself 700 wives and 300 concubines, and these many women turned his heart away after other gods (1 Kings 11:1-4). We have all heard of the wisdom of Solomon, yet his choices also show a great deal of foolishness. In spite of being king, Solomon didn't obey or heed God's warning. We also are in danger of making wrong choices if we do not heed God's warning. Our heart's condition determines our destiny. We always have a choice, and that's a very serious matter of the heart.

GOD IS CALLING TO THE LOST HEART

Many believers all over the world are aware that many times the heart will wake you up at night or early in the morning to pray or to commune with God. If you are a sinner who has experienced many sleepless nights and you've stayed awake walking the floor with a restless heart, it was probably the Lord trying to reach you. Maybe you had a horrible dream and you woke up in a cold sweat. Most likely it was a demon attacking your evil heart, and your heart was tormented and filled with fear. From our youth, each of us developed a bad heart that took us through a life of Code Red Sin, hurts, and pains. We made bad decisions to commit sin, and, as a result, received within ourselves a lost heart (Genesis 8:21). This is a serious matter of the heart.

A CIRCUMCISED HEART

For the Jewish people, circumcision was commanded of God and was necessary in order to obtain His favor (Deuteronomy 10:16). Circumcision was a central part of the law of Moses. However, once Jesus fulfilled the law, physical circumcision was no longer necessary to obtain God's favor. Rather, we are instructed regarding circumcision of the heart. Romans 2:28-29 says, "For he is not a Jew, which is one outwardly; neither is that circumcision, which is outward in the flesh: but he is a Jew, which is one inwardly; and circumcision is that of the heart, in the spirit, and not in the letter; whose praise is not of men, but of God."

A circumcised heart is a pricked heart and cut heart that the Lord is able to open up to remove sin, defilement, and wickedness. Heart circumcision is a holy requirement (Acts 2:37). God uses His Word as the tool to circumcise the heart, for the Word is quick, powerful, and sharper than any two-edged sword. It's able to discern the intents and contents of our thoughts, mind, and imaginations. Deuteronomy 30:6 tell us, "And the Lord thy God will circumcise thine heart, and the heart of thy seed, to love the Lord thy God with *all thine heart*, and with all thy soul, that thou mayest live" (emphasis added). (See also Colossians 2:11.) Circumcision of the flesh can never produce a saved, pure, and clean heart, which is why we must allow God to circumcise our hearts.

CARNAL CHRISTIANS

There is a gray area of Christianity in which people straddle the fence, remaining carnal and preferring to stay babies in Christ. The Holy Spirit is still processing these people from unrighteousness to righteousness. You may find them in the dance hall on Saturday and in church on Sunday. They still flirt with Code Red and entice Code Blue. These are lukewarm, carnal

153

Christians. Their hearts may be unbelieving in many areas, but they still show forth some faith. They sin, but they show forth some change. Much prayer is needed for this group of carnal saints—they are not lost anymore, but neither are they sanctified, and their hearts are not completely right with God. They need God's light to shine into the darkness of their still sinful hearts. Christ is the light that lightens the heart. He also builds this light within us so that we may be light and so that we will have a heart and mind like His. To have the heart of Christ, we must obey His Word. To have the mind of Christ, we must allow the Lord to direct our thoughts through the Scriptures.

ALL LOST HEARTS HAVE A CHANCE TO BE SAVED

God tests hearts daily, whether they are saved or lost. If a lost person lives to be 70 years old, the Lord has tested him numerous times, and each time his heart has failed the test. This is serious. On Judgment Day, no lost heart will be excused. The lost heart remembers its sins—past and present—and prepares the lost soul and mind for future sins. The more one sins, the more vulnerable the heart becomes to Code Red and Code Blue Sin. The saddest story that I can imagine is the scenario in which a person goes to church, faithfully gives tithes, is involved in the church, prays to God, and performs other words while still retaining within themselves a lost heart. Even Christians, when looking back on their life, will agree that their heart took them places they never wanted to go, made them stay longer than they wanted to stay, prompted them to act in ways they never desired to act, and swayed them to do things they never wanted to do.

MAKE YOUR HEART SURE

Children of God, make your election sure. Save yourself from this crooked generation. You can make it if you try. Your church must become, if it isn't already, a heart hospital for lost hearts, a saving station for the blind, and a healing sanctuary for the sick and oppressed. Oh lost heart, let me plead with you. I beg you to repent! You have a defense against Code Blue Sin.

154

Even though King David sinned and had a man killed, through his ungodly deed he realized that his heart's infrastructure did not meet God's expectations and that he was not right in the sight of God. Consequently, he humbled himself and corrected his sinful state. In Psalm 119:11, David says, "Thy word have I hid in mine heart, that I might not sin against thee." We must follow David's example. God truly takes our hearts seriously. Let's not forget Simon, a sorcerer who practiced witchcraft, who came to the apostles and received of them what I believe to be the greatest instructions for mankind in the Bible. Acts 8:21-22 says, "Thou hast neither part nor lot in this matter: for thy heart is not right in the sight of God. Repent therefore of this thy wickedness, and pray God, if perhaps the thought of thine heart may be forgiven thee." Lost souls need forgiveness for their sinful hearts, thoughts, and imaginations, and so do some believers (Isaiah 55:6-9). We all must turn our hearts over to God and make our hearts sure.

THE WORD OF GOD

The Word of God never fails, and every believer should revel in it. The moment the Word enters the heart, the heart begins to change. The more of the Word we get, the more change takes place. If you were a liar with a lost heart before the Word came in to dwell, once the Word came to inhabit your heart, you should quickly begin to hate a lie. Though you did many unholy things in the past, the Word's presence in your heart will prompt you to begin to do good and righteous things. In short, it's the Word that changes the heart from unrighteousness to righteousness. Christ spoke the Word, He was the Word, He lived the Word, and He dwells in every true believer. The Word is designed for man's heart. If there should come a time in your life when loneliness is your best friend, sickness is your cloak, sleeplessness is a nightly feast, and fear is your daily meat, open the Bible, open your heart, and dine on the Word. It will do marvelous things for you. With the Word you can move those mountains in your heart. Faith is the strength of God's Word, and love is the strength of faith. Salvation comes to the lost heart by grace through faith, and faith comes by hearing the Word. The Word comes forth from the heart of God. Nothing works in Christ without an active Word working in us. All it takes is for us to act by faith from our heart and God releases all that He has planned for us in our lives! You can't draw money out of a bank account if you have not deposited any money. However, if you deposit $110 in the bank, eventually you will have $115 available to you because of accumulating interest. The same goes for the Word of God deposited within our hearts. It pays good dividends. Satan hates the Word and devises plans designed to remove the Word from our hearts or, at the least, render it powerless (Luke 8:11-15). Never allow satan to take you on a Word fast or a gospel vacation. Protect your heart. Obey God's Word. Remember, it's impossible to obey what you do not know. Make the study of God's Word a top priority in your life. If you should find yourself facing insurmountable struggles, get in the Word, have a little talk with Jesus, tell him all about it, and thank Him that you were once lost but now you are found. Trust Him completely and worship Him, for the heart you save by doing so may be your very own.

A Deceived Heart

Isaiah 44:18-20: "They have not known nor understood: for he hath shut their eyes, that they cannot see; and their hearts, that they cannot understand. And none considereth in his heart, neither is there knowledge nor understanding [...] He feedeth on ashes; a deceived heart hath turned him aside, that he cannot deliver his soul, nor say, Is there not a lie in my right hand?"

Deception, I believe, has caused almost as much harm to the Christian church as Code Red Sin has. I believe that the deceiver will receive as great a damnation as the false teacher and the prophet. Deception just may be the greatest friend of fornication and adultery as any single element working among the human family. *Deceived!* The word carries a magnitude of remorse and hopelessness. It means "to beguile, to defraud; that which gives a false impression whether by appearance, statement, or influence."

Deception is a bait and a snare that causes much instability in the heart. It signifies error and a wandering from the right path. It deludes and beguiles thoroughly. Self-conceit can be the same as self-deceit, as both is a sin against common sense. The seriousness of the issue is that a saved heart can be deceived and bound in Code Red deception the same way that a lost heart can.

A believer can become corrupt by mingling the truths of God's Word with false doctrine, misunderstanding, and/or wicked notions. This "huckster" causes a person to go astray, to wander, and to think he is on the right track. The lust for riches deceives many people; most will quickly seek riches rather than God. Christ exposed this problem in Matthew 19:24: "And again I say unto you, It is easier for a camel to go through the eye of a needle, than for a rich man to enter into the kingdom of God." (See also Matthew 6:33.)

Lust for riches is not the only kind of lust that deceives. Lust of various kinds will betray you when deceit is the source of its strength. It has caused many Christians to marry the wrong person, buy the wrong house, join the wrong church, and believe the wrong doctrine. You may be deceived in your mind, heart, will, and desire; however, the area that's most dangerous is when you are deceived within your heart. A false idea or wrong interpretation of God's Word can cause you to sin and believe that it's still okay. Deception of the heart is a terrible state to be in because a deceived heart will also reject the truth of God's Word. If you are a habitual sinner and still believe that you are saved, a seducing spirit may be deceiving you—this is a very serious matter of the heart. Deception has very dire circumstances, and it can affect every area of life.

Perhaps you have met a non-believer and you are tempted to marry him or her, you are being deceived. He or she looks like the right one to you. You feel something in your heart. Your mind reels when you decide to get married. You are sure that this is God's will; you "feel" the presence of the Holy Spirit! You're sure that God will bring him or her to salvation in His time. One year later, though, you're sorry, and you can hardly wait to apply for a divorce because that person you married wasn't fit, wasn't God-sent, and you were deceived! In the church family, many choir members, ushers, deacons, teachers, and even pastors are still lost or saved but bound to error and deception. The heart plays the controlling part in our eternal destiny. When a deceived heart receives the truth through much prayer and deliverance, it may try periodically to rebel against God, but the Spirit of Truth will win every time. Light is stronger than darkness. God works to renew, fashion, restore, and change our deceived hearts. If He has to, He will give you a new heart. Deception is a serious matter of the heart. Galations 6:7 says, "Be not deceived; God is not mocked: for whatsoever a man soweth, that shall he also reap." And again the Lord warned us in Luke 21:8, "Take heed that ye be not deceived: for many shall come in my name, saying, I am Christ; and the time draweth near: go ye not therefore after them." We must guard our hearts against deception in every aspect of life.

The scary thing about deception is that deceived people don't realize that they have been deceived and tricked into believing a lie. When people in leadership are deceived, this is the scariest kind of deception, for they are in a position to lead others astray as well (Ezekiel 14:9). God is not the author of deception; satan is. However, God has power over all things and may allow deception to rule over disobedient, unholy, and backsliding people. The prophet Obadiah saw the truth about deception in Obadiah 1:3, saying, "The *pride of thine heart* hath deceived thee, thou that dwellest in the clefts of the rock, whose habitation is high; who saith *in his heart*, Who shall bring me down to the ground?" (emphasis added). In other words, people who pridefully boast "I'm the head deacon in this church," or "I'm the best Christian in this congregation," or "I'm God's gift to the Christian world for I am so holy" are being deceived by the pride of their own heart. Every man and woman has the power to deceive and be deceived. Deception is rarely one-fold; if you are deceived in one area, more than likely, you are deceived in other areas, too.

Deception is a very deadly thing to a true believer. Therefore, we must totally give our whole heart, mind, soul, and body to Jesus; act on the Word of God by letting it be alive in our daily lives; and gain as much knowledge about our heart as possible by fasting, praying, and keeping the doors of our heart open to God. If we do this, deception will not be our destruction (Revelation 21:27). Deception allows its victims to go through trials and troubles without experiencing the amazing grace of God. If we refuse to listen to God now, we will have to listen to satan forever and ever. Deception gives all permission to serve God in their own way, but God demands that we serve Him in His way. If we allow deception to invade our hearts, we cannot please God.

ETERNAL CONSEQUENCES

The war is on; the battle is hot and fierce. Satan sends fiery darts of deception, and the saved man retaliates with his sword, the Word of God. The saved heart, using the Word of God, wins but, unfortunately, lost hearts will eternally be vanquished to hell. "Oh Lord, I didn't know" and "My God, I'm so sorry" will be heard in the midst of the fiery flames of damnation. Hell is the eternal consequence of man choosing not to accept God's gift of salvation. In essence, man chooses his own will over God's. The term *will* in simple term means "a continued desire, a purpose, a wishing, to will." God never forcibly removes or overrides your will. There is the will of God and the will of man. When anyone truly says from within their heart "Not my will, Lord, but thy will be done," they give the Lord full permission to activate His will in their life. Thus, the believer is no longer deceived and will find himself doing the will of God. Not only does the Lord give us a new will but the hidden man of the heart must also be given a new nature, otherwise deception can creep in like a mist over the land on a cold, cloudy day. The more of your will that you turn over to the Lord, the more godly you become and the less chance deception can take a seed in your life. Be not deceived, your flesh is always open to your old will that used to dwell in your old sinful nature. Remember, your flesh is not saved and the real battle is within—between your inner man and your outer flesh man. This is a serious matter of the heart.

TURNING THE WILL OVER TO GOD

Have you totally given your will over to God, in addition to your heart? If not, deception is already working in your heart, mind, and will to slide you backwards from God. One mystery that I've seen in the church is that although some confess salvation, they still live in sin. Are there two kinds of salvation? No, it's deception working in the member's mind and soul. The answer to the deceptions of the flesh and the heart is found in Romans 8:1-4, which tells us not to walk after the flesh but after the Spirit, for Christ in the likeness of sinful flesh condemned all sin in the flesh. Keeping our minds, hearts, wills, bodies, and souls before God daily; walking in the Spirit, praying in the Spirit, and being filled with the Spirit; and having Christ alive in us is a real antidote against Code Red deception. Salvation is of the heart, and eternal life is of the heart; sanctification, holiness, joy, peace, and love are all heart conditions we achieve by repentance, truth, and freedom from deceptions. The African-American community has fought for many years to be free from the bondage of slavery. But all of us must discard the past and fight to be free from the slavery of sin within our hearts. A saved slave unto God is better than a free sinner unto satan. Once God is able to save the hidden man of the heart, He can then preserve the soul for eternity.

We are sons of God through the finished work of Christ, which He completed on Calvary and is now completing within our hearts. No matter what Christ has done for us, if we refuse to receive and believe it, we remain deceived in a state of rebellion (Jeremiah 5:23-24). When God made man a living soul, He designed the soul to be in daily communication and fellowship with Him and to daily give worship and praise to Him. Adam

fell, but Christ brought us back with His blood and now preserves us in himself, performing continual salvation from within
His dwelling place in the heart. He anchors the soul through faith
in Him; deception, sin, doubt, and unbelief cannot prosper where
Jesus is Lord (Matthew 22:37-38).

HOLY COMMUNION

Another deception in church I've seen takes place during
Holy Communion. Holy Communion must first be taken from
the heart. It is a heart-to-heart moment when you drink of the
Blood and eat of the Body of Christ. The emphasis is not
whether you have committed some great sin and have become
unworthy to partake of Communion; rather, it is whether or not
your heart is right with God. Your heart must be right with God!
Too many unsaved people partake of this sacred, holy service,
and so do too many believers whose hearts are not right and pure
before God. Never take Holy Communion with an evil, deceived,
or unsaved heart. We honor His death, burial, resurrection, and
His Blood in our hearts. If your heart isn't right with God, you
dishonor Him by partaking of this event in an unworthy manner.
Even during Holy Communion, many denominations look on
the outward appearance. For instance, they may shun the use of
wine. Let me remind you of what Jesus said in Matthew 15:11:
"Not that which goeth into the mouth defileth a man; but that
which cometh out of the mouth, this defileth the man." Like Holy
Communion, water baptism, the giving of tithes and offerings,
witnessing, and serving God all must come forth from the heart.

THE DYNAMIC, DECEPTIVE DUO

A deceived mind working in conjunction with a deceived
heart is what I call the "Dynamic, Deceptive Duo." These two
components are satan's most effective weapons deployed against
God's people. The Dynamic, Deceptive Duo leads one into
believing that he's all right in spite of living a life outside of the
known will of God. They may claim to live for God, but they
are false witnesses and have deceived hearts that will condemn
them on Judgment Day. This Dynamic, Deceptive Duo works

161

simultaneously to the demise of those who would otherwise be men and women of God, rooting them deeper into Code Blue Sin. False doctrines, preached by false men of God, work as wolves in sheep's clothing to deceive the people of God and lead them down a one-way path to destruction. False doctrine preached to those infected with a deceived mind and heart is the strength of the power of satan operating in their lives. Anywhere you find sin, you will likely find a deceived heart and mind.

Repentance, submission to the Word, daily Bible study, and humility before God are excellent weapons against deceptions of the heart. Sure, the things we see, hear, say, and feel do affect us, but the real battle is within the mind, flesh, will, emotions, and heart. You may run from sins you see with your eyes but not from the sinful desires of your heart. Likewise, you may appear divine and holy on the outside but be harboring a deceived, wicked heart on the inside. It's not the outward appearance that matters; it is the presence of Christ within. Christ is the Spirit of Truth and the gospel of our salvation.

While the Spirit of Truth goes out to enlighten man, the spirit of error (satan) goes out to deceive and defile man. The condition of a person's heart determines which one will rule in his life. 1 John 4:6 says, "We are of God: he that knoweth God heareth us; he that is not of God hearth not us. Hereby know we the spirit of truth, and the spirit of error." The spirit of deception uses error and unbelief to weaken the believer. Deception is like a giant octopus with many tentacles reaching outward to all mankind. You must have the power of the Holy Spirit working in your life by faith. You may still struggle, fight, and stumble, but with the Holy Spirit, you will not lose. In folklore we have the story of the three little pigs. Two of them were foolish and built their house with straw and wood, but the wise pig with long hard labor built his house with bricks and mortar. When the wolf came in code blue to eat all of them the wise pig was the only survivor. Likewise we must build our hearts on "the solid rock" which is Christ (Luke 6:46-49).

Another deceptive weapon active in the Body of Christ is disobedience. Disobedience doesn't become a real problem until it lodges itself in the heart (Ephesians 2:1-10). If you sow sin, you will reap sin. If you sow love, you will reap love. It's a law of nature that you must reap what you sow.

Now, let's take a giant step backward to evaluate our inward condition, repent, and cast off falsehood, error, and deception. Let's begin to do things the Bible's way. Religious deception, backed by false doctrine, will eventually render one into a state of Code Blue Death. Read the Word of God for yourself. No matter what the cost, stay with Christ. No matter how deep the hurt, hold on to Jesus. For we shall all rejoice in that great day, if we faint not.

12

REMEDIES AND ANTIDOTES FOR VARIOUS HEART DISORDERS

There are many heart disorders afflicting the Church today. But rest assured, there is an antidote for the wayward, backsliding, foolish, blind, lying, covetous, and lustful hearts. These kinds of hearts will make your world miserable. Demons and devils love these types of hearts. Love, faith, and truth toward God are the three main remedies and antidotes open to us for our use. Love and faith in action, backed by the Word of Truth, will cure these heart types and build an immune system that will last forever. If a believer doesn't walk in faith, love, and truth, he is in danger of developing any one or more of these types of hearts. These hearts' primary objective (when under satan's direction) is to break and destroy our fellowship with God and to interrupt and make our days miserable and unfruitful. Because of this, it is good to have a spiritual heart examination on a regular basis.

If you maintain a clean, pure, and sold-out life style toward God, your spiritual heart will never become clogged, blind, and weakened or full of backsliding and deceitfulness. A broken and contrite heart always produces good results when fighting off the attack of a lying, deceitful, or foolish heart. Let the love of God shine through you, not as a little light, but as a 10,000-watt bulb. But if you are ever overcome by any one or more of these hearts, you must activate and charge up your faith by acting on the Word of God. Make sure that you have the right faith in God and contain the faith of God. There is a difference. We need faith *in* God to receive from God, but the faith *of* God is needed to pull down the strongholds of Code Blue and defeat the lust of the flesh, lust of the eyes and the pride of life. Open the Word, find out what God has said concerning you, and obey all that He has said faithfully. You will find that your faith will act as a good deterrent, and love will be a strong shield for you.

A Lying Heart

A lying heart will produce a lying tongue that is hard to tame and control (see James 3:5-12). Truth, when spoken, will bridle a lying and deceitful heart. Truth makes it impossible for the lying heart to pour out its deceptions and tricks in your life. The more you speak the truth, the more inactive a lying heart becomes.

A Backslidden Heart

When you fall into a backslidden state, the Bible describes it as a dog returning back to his own vomit or a pig wallowing in the mud after having been cleansed. 2 Peter 2:22 says, "But it happened unto them according to the true proverb, The dog is turned to his own vomit again; and the sow that was washed to her wallowing in the mire." Recovery or restoration requires total submission, repentance, and a renewed commitment toward God's will. True submission, grounded by a daily confession of rededication, is excellent medicine for you to take to combat the backslidden heart. The spiritual disease that causes a backsliding heart consists of words that wound, doubt, and unbelief. If we maintain a sound heart, the attacks of the enemy will be fruitless. He can only target and attack us, but he cannot defeat us; for though we become as a victim, we are still victorious through Christ.

A Foolish, Blind Heart

It is so hard for the Lord to contend with a foolish heart. In Romans 1:21, Paul warns us about it. A foolish heart will produce blindness and darkness within your walk with Christ. You will find yourself being ignorant to God's will and plans for your life. You will become unfruitful and of no use to God. It's a serious matter of the heart. Why? Because the heart is so deceitful and complex that it may show itself as one type of heart when in truth it's another. No one can ever trust any heart except the heart of God.

Another good remedy against a foolish heart is to be seriously active within the church and community. Get busy for God. Begin to speak out against sin and the many works of satan. Don't be blind to the works of the devil. Blindness has darkened the church and the world. Lawmakers, lawyers, judges, governments, world leaders have developed foolish and blind hearts. Yet they agree with each other. They work together and there seems to be very little division among them. They unite for their evil cause. They complement each other.

Christ told us in Matthew 5:14 that we are the light of the world. In essence, we hold the answers for this dying Code Blue world system. The hearts of the people are at the root of this nation's problem. God is the only answer.

Would you like to be married to a comedian, clown or jester? Their primary job is to act, talk, and look foolishly. No one takes them seriously. Such is the Christian that has a foolish heart.

LUSTFUL AND COVETEOUS HEART

A covetous heart is easily corrected by love. Love acts upon a covetous heart as light acts upon darkness. A lustful and covetous heart desires to always get, to have, and to own at the expense of others. With a covetous heart you may easily become a thief, liar, robber, or deceiver. However, love will turn you around and cause you to become a giver instead of a receiver. God loves a cheerful giver, not a cheerful getter. This is why the Bible teaches that it's more blessed to give than to receive (Acts 20:35) and to focus upon heavenly treasures rather than earthly wealth. Matthew 6:19-21 says, "Lay not up for yourselves treasures upon earth, where moth and rust doth corrupt, and where thieves break through and steal: But lay up for yourselves treasures in heaven, where neither moth nor rust doth corrupt, and where thieves do not break through nor steal; For where your treasure is, there will your heart be also."

Satan developed a covetousness heart and was cast out of heaven. He desired to have what God had. He desired to rule and to steal God's glory. Be not deceived, whatever a man soweth, that shall he also reap. Would you care to be married to a lustful person? One who habitually lies? Of course you wouldn't, and the Lord Jesus Christ doesn't either. It's a serious matter of the heart. Beware of the lustful heart. If you sow lust, you will reap lust. If you deceive others, you will be deceived. If you lie to others, other will lie to you. You can't lie down with dogs and not get up with fleas.

All of the heart conditions discussed previously can be cured in a moment by true repentance. Repentance breaks the hold of all evil within the heart and will keep you from its power.

THE SAD AND LONELY HEARTS

The Church today is also afflicted with sorrowful, depressed, sad, lonely, vain, grieved, and down-trodden hearts. These hearts are more subtle, but they are no less dangerous to our walk with Christ. Joy and happiness are the keys to overcoming these types of hearts. To rejoice and be exceedingly glad works miraculous wonders in the heart. Humbling ourselves in obedience and total commitment to God makes the heart a solid ground for joy. When we become thankful for His mercy, grace, and truth, and when we praise Him for His love and kindness toward us, these negative heart types lose their power.

Satan sends the spirit of depression in order to gain an advantage over you. Sadness, loneliness, and sorrow are key tools of his trade. God defeats him by giving you exceedingly great joy. Joy has its strength in worship and a right relationship with God. If you are ever overcome with a vain, downtrodden, or depressed heart, it will hinder your walk and daily fellowship with God. Entering into God's presence on a daily basis is mandatory in order to combat this type of heart. In His presence is the fullness of joy. Personal praise and worship time during the week, along with reading God's word faithfully, are components of entering into God's presence. God's Word not only strengthens the heart, but it's also the strength of joy. Both joy and the Word of God act as a covering and defense from a Code Red depressed and lonely situation. Christians should also know that joy and peace bring you closer to God and draw others closer to you. Fasting and prayer are also good weapons to use against grief, loneliness, and sadness. Your unsaved flesh is vulnerable to the destroying forces of evil, allowing them to seed, grow, and multiply in the heart. If you as a Christian are attacked, go to the book of Psalm, read it over and over, and find a fellowship or assembly of God's people that really rejoice in the Lord. Spend quality time in intense praise and deep worship. Sing your favorite hymns and just get yourself happy. Christ is our joy and our defense. Go to Him, lean on Him, tell Him your troubles, and turn it all over to Him. He is a burden-bearer and a way-maker. He will be your strength and strong tower, a covering and a shield of protection. He is a shadow from the heat and a cover from storms and rain. A sad Christian can never please God. You cannot please God, magnify the Lord, or become a true witness to our fellow man while under the influence of sadness, depression, and loneliness.

Another remedy against a sad heart is to think good thoughts. Learn to control the thoughts of the mind, heart, and flesh. The Bible tells us in Proverbs 17:22 that a merry heart is like a good medicine. The many mind altering drugs used by most doctors for depressed, sad, and lonely patients are nothing compared to the power of the spiritual heart, the Word of God, and the joy of salvation. While we give medication for the natural man, sin within the spiritual heart may be the actual problem. I believe that many of the mental patients incarcerated in mental institutions would be greatly helped or delivered by receiving salvation. Losing our old mind for Jesus and being madly in love with Him is a great defense against insanity. We serve a God of joy, happiness, and glee. Are there sad, sorrowful, and depressed angels in heaven? No way. Even the angels rejoice daily. When we fervently pray in the spirit, it humbles our heart, allowing joy, peace, and faith to take seed and grow. The peace of God is given unto us through Christ. Philippians 4:7 says, "And the peace of

God, which passeth all understanding, shall keep your hearts and minds through Christ Jesus." (See also John 14:27.)

It is difficult to exercise your faith while sadness and sorrow are present and in control. Prayer is also a heart regulator that lifts you up when you are down and brings you down if you ever get too high. Deep prayer strengthens and will soothe whatever it is that ails you. Having a made-up mind and a fixed, unmovable heart toward God is a good antidote and defense for the many worldly blues that assail us. The enemy cannot toss you to and fro like the wind if you fix your heart firmly toward God in Christ. Having a made-up mind is a good shield against loneliness of the heart. Even when a loved one dies in a Code Blue situation, joy working with a fixed heart and a made-up mind will always see you through. I have seen the passing away of two wives, my mother, my father, two sisters, and seven brothers along with aunts, uncles and many friends. In times like these it was the joy of the Lord that pulled me through. Weeping did endure for the night, but joy came in the morning (Psalm 30:5).

Don't allow yourself to become trapped in the Code Red web of loneliness and sadness, for it's a miserable lifestyle in which satan works to fill your heart with one of his evil, wicked, and sinful hearts. Joy never fails when love is alive and when we walk according to the Word of God, doing the will of God from the heart. We can dance on the devil's head as the Holy Spirit holds him down, for he has been placed under our feet.

THE ADULTEROUS AND REBELLIOUS HEARTS

If you're traveling along at 75 miles an hour, it is hard to for you to see the beauty of the country side, the green grass, the trees and flowers, even the lovely birds. A proud, adulterous heart can cause you to miss God in the same way. It always makes you travel faster than you ever need to go.

The adulterous and rebellious hearts can be very tricky, for they may be both natural and spiritual. They may encompass disobedience, deceitfulness, covetousness, lying, and produce just about all types of sins that one can name. They will cause you to attempt to serve satan and God at the same time. The adulterous and rebellious hearts are huge, powerful manufacturing plants for lustful, hateful, and jealous hearts. For example, in Genesis 19:31-36, Lot's two daughters planned to give their own father wine, get him drunk, and lie (have sex) with him. The older daughter laid with him one night, and the younger daughter laid with him the next night. Both of them had babies by their own father. Similarly, in 2 Samuel 13:32, David's son Amnon fell in love with his half sister. Pretending he was sick, he got her into his bedroom and raped her. He then came to hate her. He shamed her, cast her out of his house, and slammed and locked the door. Another sexual sin is chronicled in Genesis 19:5-11, where the men of Sodom and Gomorra wanted to know (have sex) with the male angels from heaven rather than Lot's virgin daughters.

One can easily see that adulterous, rebellious hearts are clearly recorded in the Bible as far back as Abraham. But the Lord, knowing the hearts of all people, gave firm instructions to men and women, and they still stand today.

Man was not created for sin. He was created to walk with God. When man turns from God back to sin, it is like he is playing spiritual Russian Roulette. It's like trying to make a pet out of a rattlesnake or drinking poison along with your favorite lunch or dinner. The food is great, but the drink is deadly. Salvation is great, but a rebellious, hard heart is deadly. Many are deceived into believing that they can serve satan and God at the same time. Don't be deceived with this lie. The adulterous heart never closes its doors. It works overtime, paying high wages with paychecks you can never cash. Turn to Christ, repent, and be born again of the water and of the Spirit. Let go and let God.

Most other types of hearts are manifested as the result of sin, but the adulterous and rebellious hearts are actually the producers of their own type of sin. Spiritual adultery and natural adultery produce a sea of darkness within a man's heart that will soon manifest itself. The antidote is for all to turn to Christ, repent, and be born again of the water and of the Spirit (John 3:1-3).

THE STONY, HARDENED, AND UNBELIEVING HEART

A stony, hardened, unbelieving heart requires an emergency heart replacement. In scripture, God portrays these stony hearts as hard ground in which no sower can sow good seed (Matthew 13:3-23). It is nearly too far gone to salvage, and God is the only surgeon who can do the job. There is little life left. The intents, contents, and motives of the heart are locked in a sin condition. Only a new heart, along with faith, love, and hope from the Lord, can breathe new life into these Code Red and Code Blue patients (Hebrews 3:12-19, Mark 16:14, Ezekiel 11:19).

FILLING THE VOID

Every person has a void in his or her heart, which is meant to be filled with Jesus. Alcohol, cigarettes, caffeine, drugs, and food are all things that people sometimes use to fill this void. Getting high is nothing new for mankind. Taking drugs isn't new, and neither is getting drunk. There are many instances in the Bible that tell of the excess use of wine. Since the fall, man has always desired to have a spiritual experience (high) outside of God's anointing. The largest "drug" store may be found on the corner of most streets in most cities. Many illegal drugs used 25 years ago are legal by prescription today. This indicates that the illegal drugs of today will be legal a few years from now. People turn to anything except God, it seems, to try and fill the void in their hearts. The Lord doesn't mind His people being high as long as it's a result of the indwelling of the Holy Spirit. In fact, we all must seem to be drunk at times if we're truly saved. No true believer who has ever been filled with the precious gift of the Holy Spirit can say that he's never been drunk in the Holy Ghost. Acts 2:13-15 gives an example of this: "Many mocking said, these men are full of new wine. But Peter […] said unto them […] these are not drunken as ye suppose, seeing it is but the third hour of the day. But this is that [Holy Spirit] which was spoken by the prophet Joel."

Those looking upon the disciples just knew they were filled with new wine. But, they were filled with the Holy Spirit, which is a better "high" than alcohol, drugs, or overeating. You can drink coffee or alcohol or smoke four packs of cigarettes and you'll feel nothing compared to being drunk in the Holy Spirit. Man-made drugs cannot compare to the Holy Spirit. God wants all of His people so drunk or so high in the Holy Spirit that sin, sickness, and disease cannot touch them.

After satan saw the intoxicating power of the Holy Spirit, he began to seduce man to use artificial means of getting high, to bend man's will to his very own. Today, getting high has become a monster, second only to satan himself. I believe that deep within man today there is a desire to be on a higher plane than they can get to on their own. However, rather than repenting, being saved, and being filled with God's Spirit, they seek for fleshly alternatives.

Satan, knowing the weakness of man, has used the hearts and minds of men to develop alcohol, drugs, and preservatives to take man out of his natural state into a state of anti-God consciousness. This causes a false satisfaction in the heart and delays the heart from reaching out to God.

Many don't see caffeine as a drug, but excessive coffee drinkers confess that they cannot function without their morning coffee. They are addicted. Our morning cup of caffeine must not be seen as needed above our morning prayer and worship. Pre-scribed drug abuse is also legal, but it is out of control, and it has turned into abuse. Drug abuse of any kind will eventually cause a bad heart condition within that can only be completely healed by repentance, salvation, and time. The true church of God can claim a rehabilitation rate of about 90 percent, yet the states won't sup-port the church. Instead, they try to bridle the mouth of the church and its power. They continually fight against the endorse-ment of the local church as a direct avenue of deliverance. There-fore, the supreme antidote for the drug problem is denied and the use of illegal drugs increases. To be baptized in the Body of Christ, the Bible way, will change anyone's life.

The chain cigarette smoker is a drug addict just as much as the marijuana and cocaine user. Anything we put into our bodies that is not ordained by God is a Code Red Sin. The main problem, though, that is still hidden is this: all drug addicts and alcoholics have a serious spiritual heart condition. They are under satan's control and in a state of danger of being with satan in Code Blue hell.

Then there are those who are addicted to food of every kind. Many foods contain drugs, chemicals, and poisons that destroy our inward parts. While nutritional books are available to the food addict, let me suggest to you that the Bible is your best antidote for all sin and disobedience. Gluttony is a sin. Study God's Word, find out what Jesus ate, eat what He ate, and you will be delivered.

DESTRUCTIVE HEART TYPES

There are heart types that work primarily in the areas of inward desires, emotions, and feelings. Many times these hearts begin to develop at an early age and mature as the individual matures. These destructive heart types cause misery and strife to all that allow them to manifest themselves. I have been a victim. Most of the time a spiritual heart transplant is necessary, but a spiritual heart operation is always necessary. Mental health doctors, for the most part, work on a cure for the mind, never realizing that a spiritual problem may exist that can only be handled by God, the Great Physician. To give a dark heart, an atheist heart, or a workaholic heart a tranquilizer is like pouring a bucket of water on a forest fire. Many times the atheistic, dark, covetous, or workaholic heart refuses to submit or commit to any other way but their own, for they desire to rule their own lives without serving God. They remain in control of their body and their lifestyle, and they control its operations. Desiring things not of God, they set themselves up as mini-gods, believing deep within that there is no real, true, and living God.

THE STINGY, HAUGHTY, AND COVETOUS HEARTS

The stingy, haughty, and covetous hearts walk in pride, covetousness, and ignorance. Many times something terrible has to happen to bring people with these hearts to their knees before their hearts are open to hear the gospel. False joy and self-righteousness are by-products of these hearts, giving the holders a desire to go beyond normal means to get what they want. "I'll help myself," "I'm able," "I'm going to get it regardless," and "God helps those who help themselves" are the mottos of these hearts. Blind to God's ability and in doubt as to whether there is a God, these dark hearts are badly in need of the light of life in Christ Jesus. Daily reading of the Word of God will soothe these hearts more than any medicine ever could.

The Word breaks down the strong walls of these hearts and slows them down enough to be saved. Soon they become free and realize that their real treasure is in heaven, not on earth. They develop a personal relationship with God after true repentance. By relationship and fellowship, their heart becomes as the heart of Christ, willing to give above the desire to receive.

MORE DESTRUCTIVE HEARTS

Hearts that have been damaged by anger, division, child abuse, divorce, hate, spousal abuse, madness, or abortion find special favor with satan. They work in his favor daily to lift up and establish his kingdom. The relationship between satan and these hearts is clearly exposed in society today. These hearts affect the nerves, mind, and emotions. Though very unpredictable, these hearts will do unbelievable deeds. Unable to control their emotions or feelings, they can't be trusted. They seem to gather strength in number by hurting others physically and verbally. Their strength may also lie in their ability to endure pain. They are a ruling group of hearts that have the ability to kill, even though tears may be flowing from their eyes. Very hard to satisfy, they never reach a permanent place in life where joy and peace may be found, for they always exit the church in a Code Red State. Confusion, destruction, woes, and stressful situations set these hearts on fire. Angry one moment and sad the next, they produce a neurotic type of lifestyle that may keep them forever

175

from God. These types of hearts, if not given the Word of God continually, have little mercy for anyone. These heart types can be found in every city, courthouse, and jail cell. People will continue to be prejudiced against one another and cause serious conflict as long as these hearts are in control. Peace through the eyes of salvation is the key here. God's grace and mercy, once clearly understood by one of these hearts, will cause it to repent in most cases. God's perfect peace working with joy is a dynamic duo. Once saved, these hearts tend to be strong and solid, vowing never to return to their old way of life.

THE DIVIDED HEART

A divided heart may need a spiritual operation in order to be brought back into order. One day it loves; the next minute it hates. One hour it is peaceful; the next hour it is fighting in the streets. It's a very confused heart. It abuses its children and feels so sorry when it's over. This heart type has defiled the best of marriages. These hearts are very unbalanced in nature, due to the rejection of Jesus Christ as their personal Lord and Savior. Many times, just the presence of a Bible has a very positive or very negative effect on these hearts. It may become quiet at times—even still—when the Word of God is spoken.

THE ANGRY HEART

The angry heart, for the most part, is demonically controlled. Nervous conditions may be a result of an angry heart, as well as extreme high blood pressure. The angry heart, as well as the mad heart, must be tranquilized by the Holy Spirit, soothed by the Word of God, and overcome and changed by the power of God in order to be saved. Never underestimate these hearts, for without Christ they can't be trusted.

SINFUL HEARTS

Sinful hearts produce a myriad of evil works, including lust, fornication, homosexuality, incest, child molestation, and other kinds of filth and perversion. To verbally describe all of the works of these hearts would be a sin. In my opinion, it's these hearts that cause the fires of hell to burn the hottest. These hearts will cause God's wrath to be greater at Armageddon, for they trod on the Word of God and bring His creation to an open shame. These vile hearts love to use human bodies to pour out their poisonous devices. Even though they are covered in Code Red and sealed in Code Blue, they do have a sick kind of love for each other. They produce the wicked pleasures of sin as they function in the hands of God's wrath. These are they that have Jesus Christ as their bitter enemy. They are so vile, so corrupt, so abominable, and so deceitful. Yet, they are very popular to this dying world. They have changed and weakened all of the moral values written in the Word of God. Men lie with men, animals, babies, and even their own sons and daughters. They are lovers of themselves; they are perverted and rotten to the very core of man's being. The Lord marks these hearts for total destruction. The fires of hell will be turned up 1,000 degrees hotter just to make sure they receive their just reward, for they would contaminate even the most holy place. So cunning, so subtle, so wicked are they that only God's appointed servants anointed with power can overcome them (see Proverbs 6:23-33, 7:6-27, 9:13-18).

They hide themselves within the human body just waiting to attack, destroy, degrade, and hurt. They have created an arsenal of pornography and have invented many sexual abuse devices so evil that one cannot believe the heart of man could go so low. (See Romans 1:24-32 and Ephesians 5:11-12.) Even though men are nasty, mean, cruel, and corrupt, our Lord and Savior did die for them also, knowing that these hearts would one day rule supreme and destroy multitudes of souls. They tend to work together, helping and supporting one another in darkness of the night-hour behind closed doors. Devils and demons travel to and from these hearts at will.

I have seen some sinful hearts come into the church, but they reject the gospel most of the time. The gay heart accompanied by a religious spirit will find a gay church to worship in.

These heart types require massive deliverance ceremonies. They are faithful and true witnesses for satan, showing his black heart openly. They created AIDS, support the movie houses, and are in the midst of every rape case. Abortion first came from these hearts and has spread throughout the land killing millions of babies each year. These hearts have been in action for thousands of years gathering more and more in number each year.

Despite all this, God has a plan, He has a purpose, and His will is going to be done. We who are saved must bear the infirmity of the weak. We as believers must "witness" to these hearts and live holy lives in their presence, for God is not willing that any should perish.

WHAT CAN YOU DO?

What can you do about a disobedient, adulterous, hardened, proud, unbelieving, evil, rebellious, and fearful heart? Without Christ in his heart, man is prone to commit adultery, murder, lie, steal, take drugs, and even rape. Satan controls the imaginations, thoughts, and intents of millions and wants to control you too. Even though you are saved, he tries to control God through you, just as God controls him through us.

A heart full of these evil tactics are never satisfied and never will be. Their ways are the ways of Code Blue Death. They reject God's Word, say no to His will, and rebel against His holy righteousness. They are no respecter of age or persons. They are found everywhere—sitting on a park bench, jogging along a pathway in the morning sun, driving along the roadway, or even in church on Sunday. What it all boils down to is spiritual ownership: who is the true owner of your heart?

Man's only hope is to give his heart totally to God. We cannot control our own hearts. Only God has the power to change them and keep them, but God only keeps those hearts that are completely given to Him. The battle for souls is being fought within the heart of man.

178

The dangerous heart conditions we've examined in this chapter are things we should be greatly concerned about. They cause the heart to war against the spirit, soul, and body of man, to openly defy all of God's commandments, and to love darkness more than light. These heart types continually devise much wickedness. They are evil and cunning and will not be denied until God exposes and cleanses them by His mighty power.

These heart conditions ruin marriages, destroy families, and place men's feet at the gate of hell. Code Blue Death is their friend, and Code Red Hell is their partner. Indeed hell is full of those afflicted with these maladies.

These are deceiving conditions. They cause a young man to believe that he is a woman trapped in a man's body. They cause a young woman to believe she is a man trapped in a woman's body. They cause children to become runaways, to take drugs, to experiment with sex, and to become parents before they even become teenagers. They have caused many nations to make abortion a legal form of birth control. Through the sin of abortion, we have surely killed presidents, future CEO's, and pastors. We have altered America's future and purpose. With every choice there is a cost. Is this not a serious matter of the heart? Any person who has a heart like those described in this chapter is in serious trouble with God.

Do you have any of the hearts we've examined? There is only one antidote. There is only one remedy. It is salvation by grace through faith in Jesus Christ as your Lord and Savior. Protect your destiny by completely submitting and obeying God's Word. It is God's will that all hearts return to Him.

Warning! Warning! Hear ye! Hear ye! Read all about it! As you read the front page of the *Washington Post* or the *New York Times*, you will find the manifestation and works of these hearts. In Congress, the Senate, governments, and heads of state, these hearts are there waiting to take control and rule. In automobiles, on airplanes, in subways, on the streets, and in the highways and byways, these hearts are working, scheming, and planning ways to satisfy their lust for sinful desires, fame, and fortune. Without

Christ in complete control of their hearts, these people are like time bombs waiting to explode. At any moment these hearts will commit adultery or murder. They will lie, sell and take drugs, rape, and steal. These hearts are the ruling types, and they desire to control you. Even at football, basketball and baseball games, and in movie theaters, they are there bending, controlling multitudes of people to do their will. These hearts are never satisfied and never will be, for their ways are the ways of Code Blue Death. Until death is destroyed, they will continue to lead mankind astray. They reject God's Word, saying no to His will and rebelling against His righteousness. Sitting on a park bench, jogging along a pathway in the morning sun, driving along the roadway, and (sorry to say) sitting in church every Sunday morning, these hearts are there in control in some way.

These types of hearts are the most dangerous of all the other sinful heart types commonly known, and they are the ones we should be most concerned about. Why? God is angry with them every day. Psalm 7:9-11 says, "Oh let the wickedness of the wicked come to an end; but establish the just; for the righteous God trieth the hearts and reins. My defence is of God, which saveth the upright in heart. God judgeth the righteous, and God is angry with the wicked every day."

These hearts really war against the spirit, soul, and body of man and openly defy all of God's commandments, laws, and plans for man. These hearts love darkness more than light. They plan and devise their own wicked ways night and day. These hearts have so cunningly woven wickedness and evil within themselves that it takes God and all of His power working in one's life to expose their hidden plans and to correct their sinful ways. It is sad but true: these hearts have caused more souls to be lost than all other sinful concepts and hearts combined. They have ruined marriages, divided families, and placed man's feet at the gates of hell, in a deep sea of sin. Code Blue Death is a friend and Code Red Hell are partners of these hearts. Earth's graveyards and satan's hell are full of hearts such as these. Every minute, every hour, and every day, satan continues to place his seal of 666 on these heart types.

The only hope for people today is to give their hearts to God. Men do not, cannot, and will never be able to control these hearts, for these hearts will always control them. Only God has the power, wisdom, and knowledge to out-think, reshape, know, and replace these hearts. I believe that the battle that rages between good and evil, and righteousness and unrighteousness truly lies within the hidden man of the heart.

Postlude

THE DEAD THING

I shall never forget the day that I decided to visit a local, so-called "on fire," spirit-filled church that I had been hearing so much about. As I parked my car between two very expensive automobiles, I could hear the musicians playing, the choir singing, drums and tambourines beating, and much shouting.

"Oh my goodness," I said in my heart, "there is going to be a shouting time in this church today. Oh yes, this is really going to be good!" As I approached the entrance, two ushers who were wet with sweat met me and danced me to my seat. There, I beheld a lady across from me who was having spiritual spasms between two deacons who were leaping up in the air as high as they possibly could.

"Oh my goodness," I said out loud, as I viewed the pastors in the pulpit as they rocked from side to side so fervently that I thought they must be in danger of breaking their ribs or dislocating their spines. "High praises and worship are surely going on here today," I murmured to myself as I joined in by clapping my hands and giving thanks to God as loud as my voice range could take me. Finally, it was time for the preacher to preach. He tried to calm the people down with no real success. Without a text, he just started preaching, dancing, and shouting until there was just no more breath in his body. He was really good! "Oh my, this must be what heaven is going to be like," I thought as I saw the musicians swing their instruments to and fro, playing them frantically as if it were the last song they would ever play under the anointing. This went on and on, and I was having myself a good time in the Lord. Then came the altar call and about 25 people surged forth, and it seemed that they would have run over the minister if the deacons had not held them back with all of their might. The preacher laid his hands on all of them, anointing them with oil in the name of the Lord. Some fell down backward, some began leaping and dancing again, some spoke in tongues, and others gave thanks unto God in the form of a scream. There was another group of ministers trying to cast a devil out of an usher while the co-pastor gave a prophetic word over all who were still seated.

Everybody was happy as the service ended; they were hugging, laughing, and showing much joy. Many people shook my hand, saying, "Praise the Lord, brother, it's great to see you!" Yet, as I walked to my car, a strange feeling came over me. When I sat down behind the wheel, my heart immediately lost its joy. As I sat there in my car, God spoke to me in my heart saying, "*Don, do not look on their outward appearance but only unto me. Call no man or event good, for there is none righteous, no not one. Dancing in the spirit, my son, doesn't show forth the true condition of a heart, neither does preaching, praise, or worship. For I was not in the midst of all that you saw.*"

Overwhelmed, my spirit was at full attention to his still, small voice. The Lord continued to speak to my heart, and I was all ears. "*Most all of those you saw do not have my spirit, only a religious spirit. They are not mine inwardly, yet they have a form of godliness outwardly. These are wolves in sheep's clothing, workers of iniquity, twice dead with unclean lips. You must not judge to condemn them all for there are a few here who stand in my presence with pure and clean hearts. Unlike you, I am very displeased with the gathering of this people. Their need for me must become greater than their praises and worship to me. Though I am a God of second chances, I am not a God of second place. These are the living dead who honor me with their hands and lips while their hearts are far from me. They call on my name, but in their hearts they work iniquity.*" Then the Lord was silent. Immediately sorrow filled my heart; uncontrolled tears ran down my face. "This is a serious matter," I thought. These people had been going to church but had never become a part of the Church within their hearts. Though they prophesied, cast out devils, and did many mighty works, the dead thing of iniquity was locked within their hearts. I believe Christ spoke of this in Matthew 7:21-23, which says, "Not every one that saith unto me, Lord, Lord, shall enter into the kingdom of heaven; but he that doeth the will of my father which is in heaven. Many will say to me in that day, Lord, Lord, have we not prophesied in they name? and in thy name have cast out devils? and in thy name done many wonderful works? And then will I profess unto them, I never knew you; depart from me, ye that work *iniquity*" (emphasis added).

These people had an order of service that God had not ordered. They were the living dead in the eyes of God. They were God-chasers but not God-finders. They were serving God by religious principles but not from the inner sanctuary of their hearts. The dead thing of iniquity (lust-covetousness) had caused most of these religious people to be lost even while they were in the house of God. Somehow they had forgotten that God's will must be done from the heart. (See Ephesians 6:6.) A God-finder is always better than a God-chaser. In error, these people believed that they were saved and fully prepared for eternal life. They had church, but they didn't have Him. Though they were a church body, they were not yet part of the Body of Christ. God still wants a local assembly full of sinners and saints to be a group of people who seek Him above all else. God is tired of pouring out blessings more than salvation. Christ, as He walked with His disciples, addressed the dead thing, those religious people who confessed Christ on Sunday but lived in a Code Blue State during the rest of the week. Though they yet lived, Christ saw them as being dead. The purpose of our existence is not for our own pleasure, but to do His will so that He may be glorified in the earth.

Seeking God with a pure heart must be placed above high praises, and a daily relationship with the Father must be more important to us than dancing and shouting. Holy living must be sought even more than worship. Worship, praise, and prayer without God's presence is a dead thing that propels religious folks to be consumed in a Code Blue State. Living outside of God's will, purpose, and presence is also a dead thing. Christ died that we all would have power to put to death those dead things that would hinder our salvation.

THE KISS OF INIQUITY

In the Garden of Eden, there were two trees. The tree of life (good) and the tree of death (evil). One was the tree of righteousness (life); the other was the tree of unrighteousness (death). In the realm of our hearts, the tree of life represents a pure and clean heart while the tree of death represents a wicked, defiled, and unclean heart. God, who is more wise than wisdom itself, knows the ending from the beginning and knows all of His works (and our works too) from the foundation of the world. Acts 15:18 illustrates this, saying, "Known unto God are all his works from the beginning of the world." By His knowledge, God knew of Adam's fall, the flood, and even Armageddon before He ever said "Let there be light." My point is this: God didn't create sin; neither did He ever commit sin, yet the Lamb of God was slain for our sins' sake from the foundation of the world. Revelation 13:8 says, "And all that dwell upon the earth shall worship him, whose names are not written in the book of life of the Lamb slain from the foundation of the world."

I believe that this verse refers to a spiritual slaying while the slaying of the Lamb of God at Calvary was natural. Sin was the key issue in both cases. Christ saw this and said in John 19:30, "It is finished." (See also John 17:4.) The axe has been laid at the root of the tree, and our battle axe—the Lord Jesus—has finished His work on the root, source, and heart of sin (Luke 3:9; Jeremiah 51:20). The sin issue is over! Sin has no more authority over mankind. In other words, for every believer who believes—acts on and trusts in—the Lord Jesus Christ, sin will not be the problem. However, while the root, heart, and source of the sin is dead because of Christ, in the eyes of God the sin tree bore much fruit and still has many branches that lead to its heart.

Many church folks on judgment day shall be rejected, not because of sin but because of their iniquities, which separate them from God. Isaiah 59:2 says, "But your *iniquities* have separated between you and your God, and your sins have hid his face from you, that he will not hear" (also see verse 12). The monster of iniquity wraps its deadly arms around the heart and lays its evil eggs upon the core of our spirit so that when our spiritual heart pumps life into our total hidden man, we will be defiled, tainted, and worthless in the end. We have evidence of this concept in Acts 8:5-22, which tells of Simon the sorcerer who was baptized in Jesus' name. Upon seeing the disciples laying hands upon the people and filling them with the Holy Spirit, he offered them money (a dead thing) if they would give him this power. In Acts 8:20-23, we see Peter's response: "But Peter said unto him, Thy money perish with thee, because thou hast thought that the gift of God may be purchased with money. Thou hast neither part nor lot in this matter: for thy *heart is not right* in the sight of God. Repent therefore of this thy wickedness, and pray God, if perhaps the *thought of thine heart* may be forgiven thee. For I perceive that thou art in the gall of bitterness, and in the bond of iniquity" (emphasis added).

I believe that this is a great revelation for the Body of Christ today. All believers should ask for the forgiveness of their thoughts and imaginations, past and present. God is never the problem, but He is forever the answer. In Hosea 4:6, God stated that "[His] people are destroyed for the lack of knowledge." This is not the lack of the knowledge of sin but of iniquity, transgressions, of God's will, His purpose, and His requirements. Iniquity is the fruit, the branches and leaves of the sin tree that is kept alive by the thoughts, imaginations, plans, and works of our heart rather than the acts or works of our flesh. In other words, we may commit iniquity in our heart and not with our flesh.

While we know that all sin brings destruction, the Church has forgotten about the Code Blue kiss of iniquity–the inner defilement of the heart that will cause people to be rejected in the end, even though they have done many mighty works in the name of the Lord. While many do a work for Jesus, the kiss of iniquity still works within their hearts. They may rob God of tithes, mistreat their neighbor and/or spouse, cheat on taxes, be dishonest with the brethren, or lust after others in their hearts. Christ died for our sins, but He was bruised for our iniquities (Isaiah 53:5) so that we may have forgiveness for the thoughts, imaginations, intents, motives, and desires of our heart that would otherwise render all as unworthy for God's eternal presence. In Psalms 51:9, David cried out to God saying "Hide thy face from my sins, and blot out all mine iniquities." Psalms 103:3 promises that God does indeed forgive us of all our iniquities. The prophet Isaiah saw the kiss of iniquity and gave us a serious warning in Isaiah 64:6-7, which says, "But we are all as an unclean thing, and all our righteousnesses are as filthy rags; and we all do fade as a leaf; and our *iniquities*, like the wind, have taken us away. And there is none that called upon they name, that stirreth up himself to take hold of thee: for thou hast hid thy face from us, and hast consumed us, *because of our iniquities.*"

Though we are saved in Christ, the iniquities of our heart may keep us from being complete in Christ as new creatures—perfect, pure in heart, and inwardly prepared to see Him (Matthew 5:8). Having the truth, knowing the way, and having knowledge of scripture doesn't mean that one will be God-approved. Eternal life comes not just by confession of faith, repentance, doctrine, or religious belief, but by inner preparedness, perfection, and the presence of the Son of God. Many have given their hearts but not their lives to Christ and have become bound in Code Blue iniquity. Most leaders will confess that the world has become more religious while the church has become more worldly, seeking material gain above a pure, clean, iniquity-free heart. The kiss of iniquity, covetousness, doubt, unbelief, and evil thoughts and imaginations keep the Body of Christ running to the emergency room of God's grace to lay upon the tender tables of His mercy. God wants to perform spiritual heart surgery and remove the kiss of iniquity (dead thing) out of every heart. This is a serious matter of the heart.

We must also keep our hearts filled with Him. If He can't fill, then He can't save. God fills where He dwells. We must not think that the God who fills heaven and earth cannot fill our hearts.

God in us and His word alive in our hearts are our defense against the Code Blue kisses of iniquity. The wages of sin is still death (Romans 6:23), but the kiss of iniquity allows us to be dead while we yet live. The Pharisees and Saducees, who were very religious but still lost, are a perfect example of this. They had religion but not a relationship. They thought they were saved, they kept the law, they knew the Old Testament, but they didn't know the Savior or His commandments. Mathew 22:35-39 says, "Then one of them, which was a lawyer, asked him a question, tempting him, and saying, Master, which is the great commandment in the law? Jesus said unto him, Thou shalt love the Lord thy God with all thy heart, and with all they soul, and with all thy mind. This is the first and great commandment. And the second is like unto it, Thou shalt love thy neighbour as thyself." Their outward appearances were perfect, but their hearts were as filthy rags, full of vomit, iniquity, and Code Blue filthiness. (Isaiah 28:8: "For all tables are full of vomit and filthiness, so that there is no place clean.")

No more must the Church spend time trying to "usher in" the spirit of God; He dwells within us and will manifest himself at His set time. If He isn't alive in our hearts, we can leap, dance, tear up the pews, or break out the church windows for hours; we will feel great, but God may never manifest himself. God shows up to do His will, not ours. He will not manifest himself in any place where man will be given the glory and preeminence (Colossians 1:18). The modern church desperately needs deliverance from the iniquities of pride, unforgiveness, and self-worth worship. Our church agenda has led us to a spiritual self-destructive pattern of division because it doesn't line up with God's purpose. We tend to seek God's provisions above His purpose. The kiss of iniquity must not be found within our hearts. Cast down those thoughts and imaginations (lewd, evil, pictures that are written on the mind and heart) so that we can meet God's expectations of us and His eternal requirements. 2 Corinthians 10:4-5 says, "For the weapons of our warfare are not carnal, but mighty through God to the pulling down of strong holds; Casting down imaginations, and every high thing that exalteth itself against the knowledge of God, and bringing into captivity every thought to the obedience of Christ."

God must see His son within our hearts, and we must give Him all of our hearts and allow Him to build within us His kingdom, the most holy place, that our name will not be blotted out of the Lamb's Book of Life (Psalms 69:28; 109:13). Daily, our hearts must be turned to and tuned in with God's purpose and kept in a "yes, Lord" position.

Another Book
by Donald Downing

HIDDEN TREASURES OF THE HEART

Your heart is the key to life—both natural and spiritual. if you don't take care of your physical heart with the proper diet, exercise, and rest you could be a leading canidate for a heart attack. You need to take the same care of your spiritual heart—or you run the risk of being powerless, faithless, and vulnerable to the attacks of the enemy!

Hidden Treasures of the Heart explains the changes you need to make to ensure that your commitment to God is from the heart and encourages you to make those changes. Your heavenly Father is concerned about your spiritual health; He wants you to have a clean and pure heart—which is the greatest blessing of all.

ISBN: 1-56043-315-9